Colorful
Personalities

SUSAN ~
LEARN LOTS

Vantage
Publishing

Vantage Publishing

Other great books by George Boelcke:

The Colors of Leadership and Management

The Colors of Parent & Child Dynamics

The Colors of Relationships

Colors Tools for Christians

The Colors of Sales and Customers

Colorful Personalities – Audio CD

   (Available through: www.vantageseminars.com)

It's Your Money! Tools, tips & tricks to Borrow Smarter and
                  Pay It Off Quicker   U.S. & Canadian Editions

The American Financial Nightmare CD

The Canadian Financial Nightmare CD

¡Quédese con Su Dinero! Los Secretos del Crédito y la Deuda

   (Available through: www.yourmoneybook.com)

Colorful Personalities

Discover your personality type
through the power of Colors

George J. Boelcke, CCP

Vantage Publishing
U.S.: 1183-14781 Memorial Dr. Houston, TX 77079
Canada: Box 4080, Edmonton, AB T6E 4S8
E-mail: george@vantageseminars.com
Website: www.vantageseminars.com

Library and Archives Canada Cataloguing in Publication

Boelcke, George J., 1959-
        Colorful personalities : discover your personality type through the power of colors / George J. Boelcke.

Earlier ed. has title: Colorful personalities : the road map to understanding
        yourself and others.
ISBN 978-0-9784570-1-3

        1. Typology (Psychology). 2. Color—Psychological aspects. I. Title.

BF698.3.B63 2009   155.2'64   C2009-901495-5

Design & artwork assistance: David Macpherson
Edited by: Christina Heinze
Layout & typeset by: Ingenieuse Productions, Edmonton

Colorful Personalities is a registered trademark of Vantage Consulting

Excerpt from Marley & Me: Life and love with the world's worst dog by John Grogan.
© 2005 by John Grogan. Reprinted by permission of HarperCollins Publishers

Third Edition

Printed and bound in the United States of America

To

Every attendee of the Colors seminars. To this day, no seminar is ever the same as another. Thank you for helping me to help others.

Thelma Box, who's Choices Seminar introduced me to Colors, and who keeps challenging others to follow their passions and living their purpose.

Deryck Litoski (Capital Power), and Maxine Clarke (Epcor), and their Talent Development teams and staff for using Colors in such powerful ways.

Ann Zitaruk – one of the few friends a Gold needs.

Garth Warner, Dan Bruinooge, Treena Richards, and the staff of Servus Credit Union. No wonder Servus is consistently named a Top 50 Managed Company.

Contents

The Colors Self-Assessment

On the next two pages is a short assessment, with an extra copy at the end of the book. It is important to remember that this is a self-assessment and not a test. There are no right or wrong answers; just groups of words designed to identify your own preferences, values, and priorities. It is not about how others would describe you, or how you might act in any specific situations, but rather how you see yourself overall.

When you have completed the assessment, you will have a score in each of the different Color groups. Your highest score will likely best describe the dominant part of your personality. You may also discover that the detailed sections of each chapter describe your unique combinations of Colors more accurately than the assessment.

We are all a combination of the four personality types, or Colors. Think of each of them like pieces of a jigsaw puzzle, because all four are an integral part of making each of us a complete person.

Our uniqueness comes from the different "sizes" of these pieces – the combinations of our score. Some people will have all four Colors in balance, while most of us tend to have one or two scores much higher than others. There is no better or worse – only different, as each Color is equally valuable and special. Or in the words of the Billy Joel song: *"I love you just the way you are."*

Let the journey begin...

The Colors Self-Assessment

Score each group of words, for all eight questions, on a scale of:

      4 – which is the most like you

      3 – which is quite a bit like you

      2 – which is a little bit like you

      1 – which is the least like you

        (Each question can have only one score of 1, one 2, one 3 and one 4)

1. a) _____ compassion, sharing, sympathetic

   b) _____ duty, detailed, traditions

   c) _____ verbal, risk-taker, promoter

   d) _____ rational, knowledge, visionary

2. a) _____ feelings, meaningful, cooperation

   b) _____ conservative, reliable, stability

   c) _____ spontaneous, generous, action

   d) _____ credibility, focused, probing

3. a) _____ authentic, encouraging, spiritual

   b) _____ devoted, cautious, status-quo

   c) _____ surprises, freedom, short-cuts

   d) _____ inventive, principled, competence

4. a) _____ unique, sensitive, peace-maker

   b) _____ steady, planning, loyal

   c) _____ open-minded, playful, hands-on

   d) _____ curious, determined, rational

5. a) _____ tender, involved, connecting

   b) _____ lists, procedural, responsible

   c) _____ competitive, outgoing, direct

   d) _____ exploring, skeptical, complex

6. a) _____ devoted, caring, self-improvement

   b) _____ dependable, structured, belonging

   c) _____ flexible, daring, persuasive

   d) _____ independent, perfectionist, reserved

7. a) _____ intuition, sharing, positive

   b) _____ orderly, honor, rule-follower

   c) _____ immediate, skillful, active

   d) _____ theoretical, calm & cool, learning

8. a) _____ affectionate, accommodating, harmony

   b) _____ private, serious, moral

   c) _____ networking, adventure, winning

   d) _____ analytical, logical, improving

Your total score for:

a) Blue _____   b) Gold _____   c) Orange _____   d) Green _____

(The total of your four scores will equal 80)

Chapter 1

Introduction

Welcome to our journey of discovery – a journey of insights to understand and appreciate one another. By celebrating our differences, we gain a new set of glasses through which we can value and interact with each other. This is a book about you and about me – almost like an owners-manual for understanding ourselves, our partners or co-workers, parents, and kids.

Let's face it, every day we meet and interact with many people who are very different from us. They don't think like us, they make decisions way too quickly, or they seem to take forever to make up their minds. Some people want to have fun at all times, and perhaps they find it a challenge dealing with others who seldom relax and let loose. There are many people who often just blurt out a direct answer and appear oblivious to the fact that they have really hurt our feelings. Or perhaps it drives us crazy when some people want to tell us how the watch was made when we just want to know what time it is.

"Things can go horribly wrong when you
don't understand each other."
Canon Ad

Different is never about being unlovable or bad. It is simply that the majority of the world does not share our personality type. Different is not about better or worse; it is only that – different. Every Color just sees the world through a much different set of glasses, each with its unique definition of family, organization, honesty, fun, and competition, to name just a few. And each of our four Colors communicates, acts, thinks, talks, and functions in its own way.

Discovering the power of Colors results in many *"Ah ha!"* moments. Imagine how much richer and stress-free our lives would be if we just had an owners-manual for figuring out what makes others tick. What if we could obtain insights into other people's values, strengths, and stresses? What if we could learn the tools to speak the *language* of other Colors? Or what if we just spent more time looking for what we had in common – expended our energies on creating understanding and common bonds – rather than jumping into our judgments?

> *"If you talk to a man in a language he*
> *understands, that goes to his head.*
> *If you talk to him in his language,*
> *that goes to his heart."*

Author unknown – made famous in a speech by Nelson Mandela

This journey of discovery is also in large part about ourselves. For us, it begins with putting words and explanations to our many talents, joys, and actions, and also to our stresses that we have always known, but perhaps could not always define or explain. The insights and tools of Colors will open our hearts and our minds to truly understanding ourselves and others in ways we never thought possible, and ways we will utilize for a lifetime.

Personality types and the study of human behavior is not an exact science. We are always limited to general preferences and common denominators. Throughout this book are the words: majority, often, tend to, prefer, largely, and so on, to clearly emphasize that the study and understanding of human behaviors and our different personality types is not about right or wrong, or black and white.

Psychological types are also never designed to stereotype or pigeonhole. They do not put people into categories or label them. It might be easier to label, but it would be as wrong as it would be pointless. As one of almost seven billion people in the world, every one of us is unique and special. Yet, within our personality types, we do share a vast array of common behaviors, strengths, and stresses.

The true value of the tools and insights of Colors comes in using this new understanding and applying our knowledge in real life, every day. Just as no one has ever learned to drive a car just by reading a manual, growth in understanding ourselves and others involves a continuous journey.

Understanding and communicating with other Colors
in ways they value comes with huge rewards for both
them and you. It allows you to do more of what works,
and less of what doesn't, in all of your relationships.

One powerful and long-lasting way to truly understanding Colors is through a seminar with a group, office, or team. No amount of reading can replace the practicality and three-dimensional insights of a half-day seminar, and of being in the same room with each of the Color groups. It allows us to discover each other's strengths, joys, values, stresses, and motivators right in front of our eyes, in our words and actions. It creates insights that really do last a lifetime.

To have some different results
you have to do some different things.

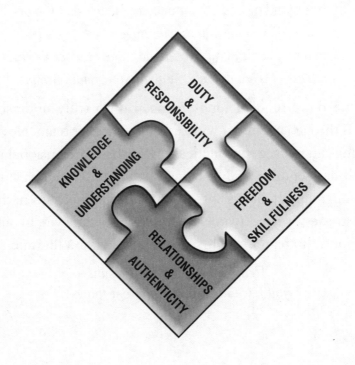

Chapter Two

The Beginning of Personality Typing

From the beginning of mankind, our species has been blessed with many talents and diversities. Among these are our abilities to think, reason, learn, and grow. Along with these come our thirst for knowledge and our drive for understanding.

Centuries ago, learning revolved mainly around survival and the need to figure out how things worked. As humankind evolved and populations expanded, it became clearer that we all have different talents and many unique abilities. Some of these are learned, while others appear to be inherent in our personalities.

Since it has always been more logical and practical for humans to live in groups, which later became communities and cities, it also increases our need to interact and to get along with each other. So for literally thousands of years we have been studying each other to create more of an understanding and appreciation for our different gifts, generally classifying ourselves into four different groups or types.

The first study of personality types dates back to the Greek Hippocrates, around 400 BC. Hundreds of years ago, astrologers began using the four elements of nature: earth, water, air, and fire. The First Nations people also believed that our natural world was created in groups of four and developed their Medicine Wheel as a powerful healing tool divided into four Spirit Keepers.

In modern times, the Swiss psychologist Carl Jung refined the study of personality types. His studies lead Jung to see repeated behaviors which he identified into patterns. He referred to them as four psychological types and suggested that parents, society, and our environment play only a small role. Jung believed that, fundamentally, individuals were already born with their natural personality types which he defined as Sensing, Thinking, Feeling, and Intuition.

Using Jung's research, Katherine Briggs completed her many years of research on the same subject. It was also her belief that the many, and seemingly random, behaviors in humans were actually very orderly and identifiable, and could be described in various categories. Along with her daughter, they developed the Myers-Briggs Type Indicator™ (MBTI) published in 1956. The basis of her work categorized temperament characteristics into sixteen specific types. Significant research and testing has proven its validity over many years. Its success and broad application greatly increased interest in personality and temperament theory in the general population, and is still widely used today.

Dr. David Keirsey, a clinical psychologist, refined the work of Myers-Briggs in 1978. Using the MBTI, and the theories of Carl Jung, Keirsey returned to the basics of classifying personalities into four base temperaments. He published his work in the widely read book: *Please Understand Me.*

Another step was the development of True Colors™ in 1979. David Keirsey was a mentor to a California teacher named Don Lowry. Lowry translated the four distinct personality types into simple language that he originally developed for the school system. His goal, and his biggest gift and achievement, was to adapt some very complex psychological material into everyday language. In fact, the introduction is sometimes presented as a stage production using actors to portray the four personality types.

One of the first uses of colors as a psychological test was developed in 1947 by Dr. Max Luscher, a Swiss psychologist. Luscher used four basic colors and four auxiliary colors in his assessments. His four base colors consisted of Blue as a calming color, Green to symbolize strong will, Red as an energy color, and yellow to represent achievement and future orientation.

From ancient times until today, the symbolism and use of colors has been associated with everything from marketing and behavior descriptions to interior decorating. Blue is the color of the sky and the seas. It is a color of warmth, representing calm and harmony. Orange is a much more vibrant and brighter color and can symbolize "look at me," or perhaps exude energy and action.

Gold is the color of one of the most desired metals throughout history. Expressions such as "the gold standard," or "good as gold," imply stability, tradition, and dependability. Finally, Green is nature's primary color and very much connected with thoughts of growth, abundance, and creativity.

For simplicity and ease of use, describing our personality types in terms of these four Colors is one of the most effective and user-friendly methods.

The power of understanding Colors yields a vastly improved communication tool and the gift, or at least the option, of seeing all Colors in a slightly different light. Something so simple really does become a powerful tool to impact our lives and our relationships in practical and measurable ways.

"I see your true colors shining through.
So don't be afraid to let them show –
a beautiful you."
Phil Collins

Don't get your feelings hurt. This is a positive. I'm going to teach you to stand up for yourself and learn to say no, Thompson!

We've done all the tests, but when she says "Code Blue" she's definitely not referring to a medical condition.

Chapter Three

Blues: Relationships and Authenticity

The drive to put their hearts into anything
they are passionate about

The focus to help others less fortunate than themselves

Appreciating the beauty without analysis

A classic line: *"Winning isn't everything – harmony is."*

A great quote: *"The best and most beautiful things
in the world cannot be seen or even touched.
They must be felt within the heart."*
Helen Keller

I believe that my most important goal in life is to touch others and to contribute in making this a better world for us all. I am unique and authentic. I value my relationships and reach out to others through my warmth, compassion, and caring. I am an idealist and quite intuitive. I look for unity and harmony and love teamwork. I am passionate in my caring and sharing with others in order to help them realize their dreams and unlimited potential, and I value playing a small part in helping them grow.

Blues are the relationship experts of the world. With their warm smile, soft voice, and great eye contact, they are naturally gifted in making everyone around them feel special and included. Their approachable, friendly manner and helpful nature are things others are easily drawn to. In any new group, Blues quickly and easily connect with others with their warm and caring ways.

It is certainly not uncommon for Blues to spend large parts of their entire day helping friends, coworkers, or clients, by listening to their needs, and truly feeling the pain of others. Seldom will they say no to anyone, refuse to lend a hand, or make their work more important than their friends needs. If one of the big questions in life is whether someone is a giver or a taker, the answer is easy for Blues.

Caring and Being Cared About

Blues naturally see the good in everyone and everything. This makes Blues excellent caregivers, mediators, and team players. Caring for others and making the world a better and softer place are powerful ways Blues make their unique contribution to the lives of others. They will always turn their spare time into time-to-spare. Because if they don't – who will?

Encouraging and supporting others is a total win-win for Blues, who know that the best way to make a friend is to be a friend. When Blues help others to succeed, they do so because it is simply the right thing to do. They intuitively know just what to say to encourage someone, or just to cheer them up and support them.

Sometimes, many times, that unconditional caring and love is hard to find, yet is so valued and critical. It is the primary reason most Blues have, or would love to have, a pet. Blues know their pets love them unconditionally and teach them so much about life. In his bestselling book, *Marley & Me*, author John Grogan describes this Blue mindset in such a powerful way:

> *Was it possible for a dog to point humans to the things that really matter in life? Loyalty, courage, devotion, simplicity, joy? And the things that did not matter, too.*

Status symbols mean nothing to him. A dog judges others not by their color or creed or class but by who they are inside. Give him your heart and he will give you his. And yet we as humans, so much wiser and more sophisticated, have always had trouble figuring out what really counts and what does not.

Communication Is Not Just the Talking Part

All Blues are gifted communicators who prefer meaningful one-on-one conversations and the chance to share their dreams and ideas in a safe environment where they will not be laughed at or judged. In conversations they ask open-ended questions in order to get to know someone. When Blues ask how we are, they really do want to know. And when they wish us a great day, we can tell it is sincere and they really do mean it.

*"A smile or a kind word costs nothing,
yet says so much, and has such great value"*

Blues are very active listeners who always maintain eye contact and often mirror the other person's emotions through their facial expressions. Where others might understand our pain, Blues will actually feel it, and they are just as willing to share a laugh or a good cry with us. In any office or group, if someone really wants to know anything about a team, ask a Blue. They will always know, because Blues listen when many people just hear, and observe while others might simply watch.

Ask any Blue person whether he or she would prefer an e-mail, a call, or a get together for coffee, and almost all will pick the chance to see us in person. Blues understand that relationships cannot be built by e-mail. Getting together with someone allows them to use their intuition and to really listen to what the other person is not saying.

In return, when Blues want to talk, they are only asking for others to listen – not to fix or to solve, but only to listen with an open heart and mind. Just this simple, yet powerful act, will make any Blue person feel special and cared for.

Just Listen

When I ask you to listen to me and you start to give me advice, you have not done what I asked. When I ask you to listen and you begin to tell me why I should not feel that way, you are trampling on my feelings. When I ask you to listen to me and you feel you have to do something to solve my problem, you have failed me – strange, as it may seem.

Listen. All I asked was that you listen, not talk or do or fix, just hear me and I can do for myself; I am not helpless – maybe discouraged and faltering, but not helpless. When you do something for me that I can and need to do for myself, you contribute to my fear and weakness.

But when you accept as a simple fact that I do feel what I feel no matter how irrational, then I can quit trying to convince you and get to the business of understanding what is behind this irrational feeling. And when that's clear, the answers are obvious and I don't need advice. Irrational feelings make sense when we understand what's behind them. So, please listen and just hear me. And, if you want to talk wait a minute for your turn; and I will listen to you.

— Author unknown

Living in Their Hearts

Blues live on a life-long roller coaster of emotions. They succeed by following their intuition, because feelings are just as valid as logic.

Information, feedback, and what they observe around them, goes straight into their heart, feeling really deeply with deeply real feelings.

All of their lives, Blues have known that their heart has information their head does not know about. Their Green friends function through logic, but Blues live in their hearts and draw on their intuition. These are the Blue's early-warning systems and decision-making processes in many areas of their lives that other Colors will never understand, appreciate, or trust. Where Blues can get off-track, however, are those times when they have not followed their intuition. After all, it is their compass in life, even if it can be a challenge to put their intuition into words or explanations that others might understand.

There is a line in the movie, *The Wizard of Oz*, that Blues sure wish were true: "*Hearts will never be practical until they are made unbreakable.*" But does a broken heart only apply to many country music songs or romance novels? According to a report from Johns Hopkins University, there may be more to it than that. In a research study, physicians studied the causes of a group of mostly older women who had developed serious heart problems after experiencing sudden emotional shock. Nobody in the study group had actually suffered a heart attack. In fact, very few of the participants even had the slightest signs of heart disease.

The physicians found that a group of stress hormones, which included adrenalin, was up to 34 times greater than normal, and on average, two to three times higher than levels reached during a heart attack! According to cardiologist Dr. Ilan Wittstein, at least 25 percent of this study group would have died without treatment.

Yet, doctors cannot understand how or why the heart of women appears to be more vulnerable than men. While doctors might not be able to explain it, could the fact that the vast majority of Blues are females be an integral reason? After all, what the mind suppresses, the body expresses. While it is always critical to rule out any physical symptoms, there is often more to it, when internal stressors may be left with no other option but to send distress signals to the body.

Countless Blues (and many Golds) find themselves in this exact position of showing physical symptoms of stress, hurt, anger, burnout, suppressed feelings of frustration, or conflict avoidance. The reason is that feelings buried alive never die, and time alone does not heals all wounds, no matter what the world may tell Blues.

The Value of a Hug

In an ideal world, Blues would much rather receive a genuine hug than a handshake. In relationships, Blues also look for quality and quantity time together. In his bestselling book: *The Five Love Languages*, author Gary Chapman describes five distinct languages everyone speaks when showing or receiving affection. Two of these love languages are physical touch and spending quality time together, which are both critical to most Blues in their relationships.

Holding hands or getting lots of hugs are natural ways Blues validate their feelings of being cared for and loved, in ways words alone could never accomplish. It is also how Blues share their affection with others; connecting with people through a soft touch on the shoulder, a warm handshake, or a caring hug. How sad that one of the greatest gifts and joys for Blues is becoming less acceptable, or more politically incorrect:

It seemed innocent enough, and was actually very moving at the time. But it took a different turn after five-year old Savanna was seen giving her friend Sarah a hug on the playground of their pre-school. Savanna's parents were called into the office to "deal" with this matter. But it was not because either Savanna or her friend thought it was inappropriate or because either set of parents had an issue with it. Hugging was simply against the rules and broke school policy in their jurisdiction.

The school policy may be right or wrong, appropriate or not. But two more kids have learned that the Blue gift of hugs, when connecting and comforting others, is somehow wrong or inappropriate. At school or at work, in church or with friends, every day Blues look for ways to make their world a little softer and more caring, because a hug is really just a handshake with meaning and feelings.

Making a Difference

Blues seek to create a better world and leave this world a better place. They are one of the largest groups of environmentalists. They hate litter, and they support countless charities with their time, money, and talents. Blues are some of the most active volunteers in making our world a better place and generally work behind the scenes in smaller groups, their church, or in their community. When Blues volunteer, it will almost always involve a people or animal connection such as breast cancer, the humane society, or perhaps their church. While the causes can vary widely, they will always be areas Blues are passionate about, and where they feel they can make a difference.

During their lifetimes, Blues travel on journeys of personal growth and self-discovery, looking to motivate and inspire others along the way. Because of their gifted communication skills, many Blues are drawn to careers in the media. With their creativity and very expressive nature, Blues are able to reach and to help vast numbers of people, and make a difference in measurable ways.

Rachael Ray is the host of a number of cooking shows on the Food Network. While a cooking show isn't a news flash, Ray has become a media darling in the U.S. where Blues are only around 12% of the population. (Compared to around 30% in Canada)

As a relatively small Colors group, few people understand the values and gifts of Blues, which has made Ray the target of many media questions wondering how she always finds a way to look at the positives of every issue, or how she could possibly be so cheerful, helpful, and upbeat all the time. In fact, Time magazine's Joel Stein called her "America's kindergarten teacher." But the feature also ended with a parting shot, comparing her to a popular girl in high school who is impressively nice to everyone, but everyone secretly kind of hates her, and who's probably a little bit phony. How sad, totally false, and very hurtful to question any Blue's motives and drive.

During her show Ray actually serves the audience herself and has a natural gift of making people feel welcome and included. Her style on the show is to chat and to genuinely connect with people without lecturing. Even outside the studio, Ray is totally accessible to her fans, loves to hug, and chooses to focus her show more around her guests, instead of celebrities. There is no teleprompter, earpiece, or cue card. She doesn't even have writers for the show – just Ray and a huge sense of being herself.

In a world of mass media, another well-known Blue who makes a difference in the lives of millions of viewers is Oprah Winfrey. Oprah stands head and shoulders above others in her gift of connecting with people through her heart. When Oprah displays emotions, or talks from her heart, it is absolutely genuine, as this Blue role model, or any Blue, finds it almost impossible to be phony or insincere.

Oprah is just one well-known example of millions of Blues who combine their eternal optimism with dreams of making a real difference. Even the theme of her former show, *"change your life television*," reflected her passion and purpose for making a positive impact in the lives of others.

In 2003, Oprah had an even bigger dream with her goal to help one million children in Africa. While that number certainly seemed unrealistic to most people, Blues believe in dreaming the impossible dream. This seemingly impossible goal turned to reality in January of 2007 when Oprah opened The Leadership Academy for Girls in South Africa. The school eventually will be able to accommodate 450 girls each year, which will easily surpass her original goal over the coming decades. Never bet against a Blue person who has a purpose, dream, or passion.

There is truly no better way to describe a life lived with purpose and meaning, for Oprah and every other Blue. However, this example is not only about Oprah. All Blues have their own unique dreams and passions. They just do not get or want the spotlight or scrutiny that comes with it. In fact, for most Blues, too much attention is more of an embarrassment than a motivator.

Giving In to the Needs of Others

As peace makers and peace keepers, Blues often go along in order to get along. At best, Blues have a tendency to bend to the wishes of others, or to the will of a group, as they do not want to appear selfish. Learning the lesson of standing up for their own needs and wants is a difficult challenge. An inability to say no or to set boundaries seldom makes sense to other Colors, yet Blues frequently sacrifice their own wishes and desires to accommodate others, to fit in, or to feel included.

A Blue's tendency of giving in and going along can make it difficult for others to notice the clues when Blues are hurting, even just before an issue may lead to an emotional outburst. Blue's overriding desire to care for others can have them feeling that standing up for their own needs is a sign of selfishness. As a result, they seldom express their own wants or priorities. This makes it critical for other Colors to be sensitive to the needs and feelings of their Blue friends.

In order to avoid conflict, Blues frequently talk around the point and can definitely sugarcoat a difficult issue. Yet, they are often quite relieved when other Colors are able to communicate in more direct and specific ways. The lesson for Blues is to learn and believe that communication requires clarity, and clarity involves telling it like it is. After all, caring about someone is not about telling them what they want to hear, it is caring enough to be honest with them – but that is usually easier said than done.

It's The Little Things

Success for Blues is about making a difference and doing something because it needs doing, not for the attention it may gather. Blues want to feel that they have an impact in helping someone. Payday for them is to receive feedback by hearing how they have made a difference in the lives of others. This feedback should be one-on-one and in-person, not through applause, reviews, or a group thank you.

Throughout their lives, Blues are the least likely Color to choose a project or job for the money. Of course, their bills and financial needs are no different than anyone else's. Groceries and gas do not cost less for Blues, yet money is seldom one of their primary motivators. "*Can I make a different here, will I feel included and be part of a team?*" are much more important questions and decision makers, as well as deal-breakers. Having more money is great, but their focus is on what the money will allow them to accomplish. When Blues are passionate about a career or a project, a little piece of their heart goes into everything they do. Blues do not go through the motions without emotions.

Even when a Blue person sends a card or a special note, there is almost always a little something extra with it. It might be a sticker, something drawn on the envelope, or something tucked inside. It is not just a card – it's a Blue person connecting with the recipient! The challenge for Blue's friends, family, or coworkers is to understand and acknowledge the little touches and special ways Blues use to make a difference.

"Don't look for big things,
just do small things with great love."
Mother Teresa

When Feelings Can Get In the Way

When life revolves around feelings there is often a downside. Blues are deeply affected by criticism, harsh words, and cruelty. Their strong desire for peace and harmony at all cost does have a price. It makes Blues quite sensitive to any conflict or injustices. These inequities go against everything they believe in and fight for, and create significant stress. It is why Blues can often interpret criticism as a personal attack, no matter how carefully worded it may be.

In those instances, Blues will forgive, but will seldom forget. They can become more quiet, withdrawn, or resentful, but will seldom verbalize their hurt feelings. Yet, when this happens, how can there be a future when the past is always present? Unfortunately, this can become a catch-22 situation since forgiveness is not a feeling, but a decision. The other person likely has no idea what happened, or has moved on a long time ago. Yet, with a mindset to forgive but not to forget, Blues will continue to ingest poison, hoping the other person gets sick. To avoid conflict, they choose not to make waves or to speak up and verbalize their feelings, even if they may be dying inside. Sometimes, many times, other Colors really do need to listen to what Blues are *not* saying.

Blues cannot tell their heart what to think and there is no on-off switch to their feelings. Helping others is a great way Blues build their self-esteem. It is second nature to Blues who would never stop to wonder what's in it for them. Yet, Blues can get caught in a cycle of wondering what else, or what more, they could have done, instead of focusing on the huge positive impact they actually did make. Often, and almost always incorrectly, someone else's failure can become their failure.

Teamwork Makes the Dream Work

With the Blue drive for genuine relationships and harmony, working as part of a group or a team is one of their natural gifts. Always being sensitive to the needs of others makes Blues great team builders where everyone feels special and part of the group or team. They are strong believers in fostering an environment of inclusion, and they work tirelessly to create a positive and supportive atmosphere. Blues always live and believe that we really can do anything, and achieve great things, if we just do them together.

This fall, when you see geese heading south for the winter flying along in "V" formation, you might consider what science has discovered as to why they fly that way.

FACT: As each bird flaps its wings, it creates an "uplift" for the bird immediately following. By flying in a "V" formation, the whole flock has at least 71% greater flying range than if each bird flew on its own.

LESSON: *People who share a common direction and sense of community can get where they are going more quickly and easily because they are traveling on the thrust of one another.*

FACT: *When a goose flies out of formation, it suddenly feels the drag and resistance of trying to go it alone. It quickly gets back into formation to take advantage of the lifting power of the bird in front of it.*

LESSON: *If we have as much common sense as a goose, we stay in formation with those headed where we want to go. We are willing to accept their help and give our help to others. It is harder to do something alone than together.*

FACT: *When the lead goose gets tired, it rotates back into the formation, and another goose flies to the point position.*

LESSON: *It is sensible to take turns doing the hard and demanding tasks and sharing leadership. As with geese, people are interdependent of each others skills, capabilities and unique gifts, talents, or resources.*

FACT: *The geese flying in formation honk from behind to encourage those up front to keep up their speed.*

LESSON: *We need to make sure our honking is encouraging. In groups where there is encouragement, the production is much greater. The power of encouragement (to stand by one's heart or core values and encourage the heart and core of others) is the quality of honking we seek. We need to make sure our honking is encouraging and not discouraging.*

FACT: *When a goose gets sick, wounded or shot down, two other geese will drop out of formation with that goose and follow it down to lend help and protection. They stay with the fallen goose until it dies or is able to fly again. Then, they launch out on their own, or with another formation to catch up with their flock.*

LESSON: If we have the sense of a goose, we will stand by our colleagues and each other in difficult times as well as in good.

– From a speech by Angeles Arrien and based upon
   the original research of the naturalist, Milton Olson.

Since Blues draw significant energy and purpose from being part of a group, working in isolation can make them feel punished. Blues truly love to feel they are needed and included. Their desire for teamwork shows in their strong ability to share the work and certainly the credit. Blues avoid being the star and the center of attention, and any recognition is quickly and readily shared amongst their team. By clearly putting others before the tasks at hand, Blues admit that staying task-oriented, organized, or making paperwork a priority, can be a real challenge at times.

What Not To Say?

In the heat of a discussion or when making a decision, Blues want others to understand how passionate, important, or serious something is. With a coworker, friend, or often their partner, there are two statements which seldom contribute to reaching closure, or an answer with Blues:

Whatever you want: With this response, others are likely attempting to extricate themselves from something or other. Perhaps they are really giving up and would like to get back to whatever they were doing. That would be a mistake, as Blues would feel that this decision, whatever it may be, is not viewed as important and…it really is! Blues look to others for an opinion or an answer, to validate that others do care, or really are listening. Perhaps other Colors are wishing Blues would just stop talking about it, but they are going about it the wrong way and making things worse. Blues will often talk until they feel they have been heard, and cutting them off will not achieving that goal.

You are overreacting: Wrong. It is likely that a Blue is very passionate about an issue, because Blue feelings do run deep. Perhaps their strong sense of intuition is guiding their reaction right now. Or maybe their feelings are hurt and the other person does not seem to be "getting it," or understanding how important, or hurtful something is. Yes, smaller problems sometimes get blown out of proportion to their real size. But this may not be the best time, or the best way, to have a Blue see another view of 'reality.'

What You See and Hear From Blues

Blues are always open and caring, warm and friendly, and have a natural way of connecting with others. Blues have pictures of family and pets around the office, probably on their fridge, and throughout the house. They have a constant animated facial expression and are very active listeners with a gift of getting people to open up and to share.

When listening to Blues, they express lots of emotions in their voices and often use feeling-type words. They use humor and laughter in conversations and ask many open-ended questions to encourage others to express themselves with more than yes or no answers. Blues really want to get to know someone and express lots of empathy and caring in their tone and speech. Everyone quickly notices their soothing voices and calm, welcoming, and enthusiastic tones. They will also seek to smooth things over and often say *"I'm sorry"* – even when they are not at fault.

Now I Understand...

You give and give and can frequently run on empty. I need to learn to be sensitive to your needs and be aware that you have a hard time saying no. You are a loyal friend, a great partner, someone I love spending time with. You keep dreams and possibilities alive and always look for the good and the positive in everyone and everything.

I understand that when you talk I don't need to fix. I just need to listen in the same caring way that you always do. Not judging, not fixing, and not being critical – just listening. Because you open your heart so often, so easily, I need to always be mindful to step gingerly.

I want to help you choose ways to take care of yourself. After all, it is only when you take care of yourself that you can take care of others.

Almost everything you do has a little piece of your heart in it. A little part of you is in every project and conversation, and in many other areas of your life. You value putting your heart into everything you truly believe in.

You have a great sense of intuition. You listen to it and follow it and you are right more often than not. It also means I don't have to put on an act, I can always be myself, because you will not reject the real me.

I marvel at your ability to connect with others so easily in spiritual and meaningful ways. You don't just define the word friendship – you live it through your words and actions every day, all day.

Finally, I will remember that your hug or a warm touch cures many things and touches others in special, caring ways.

I am your boss or your friend. I am your partner, someone you work with, or your relative... and now I understand you a little better.

Common Blue Strengths

Authenticity
Caring for others
Creative
Devoted
Empathetic
Flexible
Friendly
Good listeners
Honest
Intuitive
Like to laugh… and cry
Loyal
Positive & eternal optimists
Sincere & genuine
Spiritual
Tactful
Totally people-oriented
Won't let others down

Bringing joy to others
Compassionate
Democratic
Easy going
Everyone has potential
Forgiving
Generous
Great huggers
Include everyone
Kind hearted
Loving and romantic
Peace-makers
Sensitive
Smooth things over
Sympathetic
Team-builders
Trustworthy

Common Blue Stresses

Arguments or conflict
Can't say no & burnout
Conflict & disharmony
Deadlines
Feeling not having done enough
Frustrated by inflexibility
Knowing we'll get hurt again
Lack of warmth or humor
Missing romance
Not taken seriously when emotional
Office politics
People without integrity
Reviews – giving & getting
Square pegs – round holes
Unappreciated
Worrying about others' problems

Cannot please everyone
Cold people
Criticism & harsh tone/voice
Domineering people
Feelings hurt easily
Intuition can cause problems
Lack of empathy or hugs
Lingering conflict/disharmony
No eye contact
Not making time for ourselves
Paperwork
Phony people/pushy sales people
Silent treatment
Unable to save the whole world
Work before people

I can understand how losing your to-do list is stressful.
But you'll make a new one by tomorrow at the latest, I promise.

Maybe we will be off this island by Friday. It's great that
you're always so reliable, but was it really necessary to kill
the cell phone battery cancelling your appointments?

Chapter Four

Golds: Duty and Responsibility

The drive to plan the work and work the plan

The focus on finishing one thing at a time before moving on

Prefers to plan and execute

A classic line: *"I know I'm right – it's either black or white."*

A great quote: *"You're one of them aren't you?*
You're a rule follower!"
Amos (Ben Kinsley) The Assignment

I believe in following through on commitments and having
others know that I am dependable, prepared, and punctual. I
am very loyal and understand what is right and wrong in life.
I strongly value my home, family, and traditions. I am a faithful
and caring friend who values helping others and fulfilling my
sense of belonging. I plan things out properly and follow orderly
and concrete steps to see things through to completion.

Golds are the largest Color group and seem to take the workload of the world on their shoulders. Whether they have been asked or not, the way Golds see it, somebody needs to do it. They believe that, *"if it is to be, it's up to me."*

Their strong sense of duty makes Golds among the most loyal and long-term friends or employees, and the largest group of volunteers. In fact, Golds and their Blue friends make up more than two-thirds of all volunteers. Giving back and lending a hand are great self-esteem builders and are just the right and proper thing to do.

Whatever their task or commitment, it will always be done in a businesslike manner, without fanfare. They are often impatient to get started, rather than sitting around talking about it.

Golds are very supportive and trustworthy with a strong dedication in all of their relationships. Even at work, they are some of the most loyal employees who will probably give two week's notice should they win the lottery. Rightly or wrongly, Golds draw a large part of their purpose and sense of identity from their work. Whether as a stay-at-home parent, an employee at work, or serving as a volunteer, feeling needed with a sense of belonging, are integral parts of the Gold identity and purpose in life.

Like a Rock

All Golds take their responsibilities very seriously. Their word is their bond and they will go through fire to ensure they keep it. No excuses or cop outs – no matter what. It might overload them and perhaps they should say no, but that becomes a lesson for next time. At the time, when Golds give their word, they will honor it, no matter what.

Like a Rock is a Bob Seger song which has been used in hundreds of Chevy commercials for many years. Since companies market to specific personality types in their advertising, nothing describes Golds better, or targets them more effectively than the title of this song. Since Golds are the largest Color group, when an advertiser like Chevy (and Golds themselves) finds something that works, they stick with it.

Chevy often uses a voice-over to describe their trucks as long-lasting and dependable. However, there are many more adjectives, either expressed or implied in the song, which apply so accurately to

Golds: solid, steady, not going to let you down, reliable, there for you, count on me, true to my word, tough, stable, dependable, and many more.

> *Mark agreed to help out with a school fundraiser for his daughter. It was not the best timing in his busy life, but his strong sense of obligation made it difficult to say no when he was asked. Yet, half way through the project, it seemed as though most of the committee had abandoned Mark. With his Gold challenge in asking for help, more and more of the work landed on his shoulders. After all, he had given his word to chair the committee and he would see it through. The event was going to be a success and it WOULD get done on time, on budget, and raise the money the group had set as their goal. None of those were optional, and neither Mark, nor any Gold, would accept any excuses, quit on the project, or refuse to take on the additional work in order to make it happen.*

> *The project was becoming quite stressful and more and more like a full-time position. But there was a job to do and he was going to honor the commitment and keep his word. Of course, the fundraiser went incredibly well. All the details were taken care of, the evening ran smoothly, and Mark felt on top of the world, yet totally run down and tired.*

The Never-ending To-Do List

Golds love making lists – everywhere and for every occasion. Lists are an ever-present reminder and guide of what still needs to be accomplished and an essential tool for success. Ask most Golds what they would do if they remembered something after they had gone to bed? Most would get up and make a quick note, and many would have some paper and pens in their night tables. With their unwavering sense of responsibility, if Golds did not write down what they remembered, they probably would not be able to relax or go to sleep. They would constantly be thinking, *"don't forget… don't forget…"*

"On the way home from a trip, I jot down the packing
list for the next one. Then when I'm unpacked,
I pre-pack what goes with me the next time."
Tim Finchem, PGA Tour Commissioner

The joy, however, is not in adding to this permanent list. The satisfaction is getting everything finished and crossed off their to-do list. That is a Gold definition of fun. When they are in control of scheduling work, based on their priorities, life unfolds pretty smoothly. Where the Gold stress level increases are the times when unexpected work shows up, or when they are asked to change their set plans or routines.

This mindset makes Golds highly efficient, if not always very flexible. Should their spouses need help, it may have to wait until Golds have finished cleaning up the garage. For a meeting, Golds want to know what will be discussed and who has the agenda, along with ensuring the meeting ends on time. And, if their credit card bill arrives in the mail today, it will get paid tonight or tomorrow. True, it wasn't due for another week, but it is simply one more thing handled, off the list, and out of their hair.

To stay efficient and on-track, Golds look for options, and value a bottom-line approach. This ranges from buying a product, attending a meeting, and functioning in their job. However, they do not like being told what to do. They seek practicality and getting on with things as efficiently and quickly as possible in order to reach closure and put one more issue or project behind them.

*A survey by OfficeTime of administrative professionals,
the majority of whom would be Gold, asked what
were the biggest time-wasters in the office:
27% responded it was meetings that went too long
26% felt it was unnecessary interruptions
21% thought it involved too much socializing
21% stated it was a disorganized work area*

Learning to Do Nothing and Enjoying It

Golds love getting through their seemingly endless to-do lists. Until that happens, they can appear to be in perpetual motion, always doing something instead of nothing. Only when their work is done, will Golds give themselves permission to play and to have fun. Until then, just relaxing can somehow seem irresponsible when there are still things that need to be done, prepared, cleaned, straightened-out, or put away. Relaxing, like having fun, is something to be earned at the end of their to-do list. But right now, there is probably just one more thing that needs to be done…Don't worry – be happy? Not likely.

The simple fun and pleasure of doing nothing is somewhere between irresponsible and impossible. Ask any Gold what they would do if they spotted a piece of lint in the living room while watching television? Other Colors might not see anything, but Golds are usually scanning the room for a crooked picture or something out of place. Would they ignore it, pick it up during the next commercial, or pick it up right away? Golds have just never fully learned or embraced the simple art of doing nothing. Of course, they relax and have fun like everyone else, but it usually still involves some kind of task or planned activity – anything that is something, instead of nothing.

Planning the Work and Working the Plan

Golds are driven to do the right thing, the right way, on time, and according to plan. After all, preparation breeds confidence and the devil is in the details. Staying on task, on-time, and efficient, are incredibly satisfying and a fixed part of their comfort zone. Whether they are organizing a party, or handling a project at work, Golds want to do it right, ensure that no details are too trivial, and that nothing falls by the wayside. They will start a file, do an outline, plan a timetable, gather their resources, and work diligently until the task is completed.

If it seems Golds are not having much fun, that is not true at all. There are simply no points for effort, or credit for attempts – results are what matter. Fun is for after work – right now they have a job to do. Golds have given their word, they know others are relying on them, and often feel as though the world is watching them. Without doubt, Golds are the steady and consistent stabilizers who keep the world out of chaos and watch all the details.

First, however, there needs to be a plan which covers all the details before Golds even get started. It would be quite irresponsible to just get going, only to discover later that they are off-track and all that work was just a waste of time. A proper outline, detailed instructions, and an agenda are tools Golds have valued since school. Many years ago as kids, they already looked towards agendas and report cards to assure they were doing a good job and completing assignments according to the instructions. It was also when Golds first learned to ask many detail-oriented questions such as, exactly how many pages does the book report need to be, should it be double spaced, when is it due, and would it count towards their grade?

One of the great strengths of Golds is designing plans, systems, and procedures. Once a plan has been made and used successfully, it remains efficient to keep this template for future use. If it's not broken – don't fix it. Plus, keeping the structure in place will speed up the process next time and allow Golds to continually increase their efficiency. To Golds, there is great safety and satisfaction in established routines and predictability, which is not subject to fluctuation or the need to reinvent the wheel.

Better Late Than Never? Better Never Late!

Planning and organizing necessitates staying on time, all the time. "You're late, you're dead," is their mentality. Being on time is not optional, and Golds are just as hard on themselves as they are intolerant of others on this issue. One of the biggest ways to honor and respect Golds is to be on time – every time. A 2 P.M. meeting means 2 P.M., not 2:10. Perceived or real, ten minutes late sends a clear message to Golds that the other person does not value or respect them.

> A well-known multi-national corporation in Vancouver, British Columbia is owned by a very high Gold. Whether legend or fact, the story of how managers meetings are conducted has been circulating for years. Apparently at the exact time these meetings are to start, the boardroom door is locked. Anyone late would simply be unable to attend and then terminated from the company. Only once did a manager who arrived late actually take an axe from a nearby fire extinguisher box and break through the locked door. His ingenuity was rewarded by being allowed to attend the meeting – and to keep his job.

The perception that others are wasting their time is a big stress for Golds. Line-ups or broken promises, excessive small talk, or meetings with no agenda, inefficiencies, lack of organization, or changing decisions are all time-wasters which can drive Golds crazy.

A powerful way to honor Golds in business, or as friends, is to under promise and over deliver. An unexpected surprise is to receive a call that their order is ready early or that their car is fixed ahead of schedule. It is one of the most simple and powerful ways for any business to retain this largest group of clients. Unfortunately, Golds know this rarely ever happens. A great trust builder in honoring Golds is to be on time and to deliver as promised. Their mindset demands no less, and it is not something Golds will easily compromise or forgive.

> *"(Even back in school) I liked being smart. I liked being on time, and I liked getting my work done."*
> Michelle Obama speech to a London Girls, School

One Thing at a Time

Golds are very efficient and skilled time-management experts who work accurately and with a single-minded focus towards deadlines and completion of tasks. The vast majority of Golds work best when dealing with one thing at a time and prefer to get a task completed, before moving on to the next job. It allows Golds to focus on the job at hand without getting sidetracked or interrupted.

While they are dedicated and cooperative team players, Golds generally prefer to do specific projects from start to finish. It allows Golds to be the quality control experts and to assure that any job is done to their high standards, when promised, and to their satisfaction.

It is easiest to picture the mindset of Golds to that of a timer. When they have taken on a task, their mental timer has started. Whether deadlines are external or self-imposed, there is (preferably) only one timer. Until that particular task is completed and the timer has re-started, they are committed and focused. Golds will readily admit that a number of projects on the go, or various "gotta do" things coming at them, are surefire ways to increase their stress levels.

One Gold who proudly proclaims her desire to single-task is author and TV personality Suze Orman. *"I, more than anybody I've ever met, do not believe in multitasking. I think it's the absolute ruination of the perfection of a project."* Orman is very proud of her ability to totally stick to her agenda and plan. *"All I care about is what I do, and I do absolutely nothing else while I am doing it."* She won't answer the phone when she is writing and has a cell phone that is never powered on.

When Orman hires people to work on a project, she insists on that same total focus from others. In an interview with Time Magazine, she shared that others may be able to multitask, but it cannot be on her time, believing that those who do multitask, accomplish mediocre work at best.

While her comments can seem harsh to other Colors, Golds value staying in control and see most issues from a black and white, right or wrong perspective.

> *"I do one thing at a time. I do it very well,*
> *and then I move on."*
> Dr. Charles Winchester – M.A.S.I I.

Living In the Next Moment

If Oranges live for right now, Golds live with an eye on the next moment. Golds always think ahead to anything that has yet to be done, could go wrong, needs to be finished, planned, or ordered. There will always be a plan B. This lets Golds be prepared and ready should something go wrong (or more likely when), and have a backup plan – just in case. It is not just a scout motto; it's a Gold core value.

Ask any Gold when they are most likely to start stressing about an important project. At 10 A.M. when they agree to take on a job, or closer to 4 P.M. when the job is due? Almost all Golds will admit it is usually right after 10 A.M. when they start planning and worrying how to get it done, what is involved, and how to assure it will get finished on time.

"Could you just enjoy the moment? Would you please
just live for what's happening right now
and not time travel to the next!"
Danny Tripp – Studio 60

The Gold drive and concern about the future, or focus on the "what ifs" in life, is frequently misunderstood. Because of what Golds plan often turns out well, others often don't even notice the amount of effort Golds have expended to assure that it happens. The Gold mindset is not about being negative. They always hope something turns out for the best, but do anticipate potential pitfalls. Is all that Gold planning, thinking ahead, and preparation worth the effort? Do other Colors appreciate their values? You decide:

Red roses were her favorites, her name was also Rose. And every year her husband sent them, tied with pretty bows.

The year he died, the roses were delivered to her door. The card said "Be my valentine," like all the years before. Each year he sent her roses, and the note would always say, "I love you even more this year, than last year on this day. My love for you will always grow, with every passing year." She knew this was the last time that the roses would appear.

She thought, he ordered roses in advance before this day. Her loving husband did not know that he would pass away. He always liked to do things early, way before the time. Then, if he got too busy, everything would work out fine.

A year went by, and it was hard to live without her mate, with loneliness and solitude, that had become her fate. Then, the very hour, as on Valentines before, the doorbell rang, and there were roses, sitting by her door. She brought the roses in, and then just looked at them in shock. Then went to get the telephone to call the florist shop.

The owner answered, and she asked him if he would explain, why would someone do this to her, causing her such pain? "I know your husband passed away, more than a year ago," the owner said, "I knew you'd call, and you would want to know. The flowers you received today were paid for in advance. Your husband always planned ahead, he left nothing to chance. There is a standing order, that I have on file down here and he has paid, well in advance, you'll get them every year. There also is another thing that I think you should know. He wrote a special little card…he did this, years ago. Then, should ever I find out that he's no longer here that's the card that should be sent, to you the following year."

She thanked him and hung up the phone, her tears now flowing hard. Her fingers shaking as she slowly reached to get the card. Inside the card, she saw that he had written her a note. Then as she stared in total silence, this is what he wrote: "Hello my love, I know it's been a year since I've been gone. I hope it hasn't been too hard for you to overcome. I know it must be lonely, and the pain is very real. Or if it was the other way, I know how I would feel.

I know it's only been a year, but please try not to grieve. I want you to be happy, even when you shed your tears. That is why the roses will be sent to you for years. When you get these roses, think of all the happiness, that we had together and *how both of us were blessed. I have always loved you and I know I always will. But my love, you must go on, you have some living still. Please…try to find happiness, while living out your days. I know it is not easy, but I hope you'll find some ways. The roses will come every year, and they will only stop, when your door's not answered when the florist stops to knock.*

He will come five times that day, in case you have gone out. But after his last visit, he will know without a doubt. To take the roses to the place, where I've instructed him and place the roses where we are – together once again."

James A. Kisner – adapted and used with permission

Tried, Tested, and True

Golds are creatures of habit who enjoy the safety and security of routines – and the reason they stay loyal to their bank, dry cleaner, favorite coffee shop, or grocery store. It is very likely they have dealt with these businesses for many years because of a combination of good service, kept promises, and value for their money. Yes, Golds are quite conservative financially, some even say cheap. They certainly want a good deal, but also know the difference between the sweetness of a cheap price and the bitterness of bad quality.

If Golds need to change retailers, they can be somewhat sad and uncomfortable. Sad, in that they can no longer rely on that business after all that time, and quite uncomfortable having to shop around for an alternate business to start all over again. Companies who understand Colors know that Golds are their largest source of loyal repeat business. Yet most do not understand or appreciate that Golds will readily voice their displeasure about sub-standard service, broken promises, and price issues. Stonewalling, getting defensive, blaming, or ignoring Golds' feedback, is a sure-fire way to lose a ton of business very quickly. When companies acknowledge a problem, apologize, or make amends, Golds will become even more loyal. Stuff happens, and Golds care enough to share feedback, because they actually want to stay loyal.

Like everyone else, Golds have a favorite restaurant. But it might take a few minutes to think of a second or third favorite. The next question to ask is, what do they normally order? The answer comes very quickly, because Golds likely already know what they are going to eat. Why take a chance on something new? They will probably order their same usual entrée. Since it's their favorite, they know what to expect and their meal will taste great. While others are impressed that Golds can decide so quickly, that is rarely the case. They have mulled that decision even before getting to the restaurant. Looking through the menu often just becomes the polite thing to do.

Understanding the Gold need for stability makes it imperative for others to be aware of Gold's apprehension about extensive changes in routines, procedures, or structures. Successfully accomplishing significant changes requires patience and open communication over an extended transition period.

Golds prefer to have some options and input before buying-in to any changes. They value clear outlines of the reasoning, benefits, and time-lines behind these changes. Simply pushing changes through can become a noticeable stress and may lead to significant backlash and resistance, both in their relationships and work lives. It may not seem logical, but there is safety in the routines of their worlds. Moving to a different place, or perhaps a job promotion to a different city, might be a good thing on the surface, but will still be quite stressful.

A Special Gold Stress

Golds know they are strict rule followers. Therefore, it stands to reason that following all the rules will result in everything unfolding according to plan. Golds believe that doing the right things should lead to successful outcomes. This applies to their relationships and kids, just as much as their attitudes at work.

> *"I skipped one class, once, in my entire four years of*
> *college, and I just sat there outside the building*
> *where the class was being held, feeling guilty.*
> *But I just wanted to rebel one day."*
> Dr. Laura Schlessinger

When Golds live their lives "by-the-book," it creates a sense of safety and security. If they play by the rules, everything will turn out as anticipated. After all, does four plus four not always equal eight? Life, however, does not always unfold as predictably as a simple math equation. Golds still get divorced, laid-off, or have bad things happen to them. When Golds have followed all the rules, and things still don't turn out the way they had anticipated, they can be facing a difficult reality.

During stressful times, the Gold mindset can default to thinking that they need to work harder, do more, get more organized, get better focused, or retreat into more cleaning and tidying up. Things will get back on track and life will turn around if they just do "more." It is a common Gold reaction in times of trouble, in hoping that their hard work, focus, and dedication will see their way through bad situations. While that approach seldom works, since doing *more* is not the same as *better* or *different*, it is a common Gold default way of dealing with stress or problems.

First, We Clean Up

Before starting any work, or even before feeling relaxed at home, Golds first need to clean up. They usually cannot focus or concentrate unless they have taken a few minutes to get organized. From their desks to their closets, their garages, or kitchen counters, Golds are almost allergic to anything messy or disorganized.

After a dinner party, Golds will probably start to clear the table and load the dishwasher. They are not signaling or hinting the get-together is over, but are simply acting out their natural drive to clean up before they can relax and enjoy the rest of their evening. Even if Golds hire a cleaning person, most will likely do some of the cleaning in advance. (*"I wouldn't want anyone to think I'm messy."*)

In their homes, Golds use a lot of shelving, many boxes to organize their garage, and really love Ikea or The Container Store organizers. There is definitely a place for everything and everything in its place, and few things are more satisfying. Other Colors may not notice or care, but for Golds it is very calming and relaxing to have their world neat and tidy and *this* is not open for debate.

At work, Golds have this same mindset when it comes to their workbench or desk, where their tools will be in their proper place, or their paperwork in neatly organized piles. For Golds to be neat, clean, tidy, and organized creates a strong sense of calm and control in their worlds, and over their work. But can this be taken too far? At Audi's headquarters in Herdon, Virginia, all employees must have their desks paper-free at the end of each day. "Spotlessness is happiness. I've always liked keeping things tidy," was the quote from an Audi V.P. to Fortune Magazine. Other companies, whose culture is very much of a Gold environment, including General Electric and UPS, have similar policies, but in the form of goals, not mandates.

Don't Touch My Stuff

From the clothes they buy to the cars they drive, Golds take pride in their possessions. Their attitudes are that these things are expensive and need to last a long time. Not wanting to spend money over again is the reason Golds keep their vehicles for many years and often dry clean many of their quality clothes.

The Gold pride of ownership has them in conflict when others ask to borrow something. In fact, they hope others never ask at all. While Golds have a hard time saying no, they are reluctant to lend most anything to anybody, or even share something from their desk at work. Golds take very good care of their possessions and believe that many people just don't share that same attitude. Plus, Golds get frustrated when something is not returned promptly, even though they have a hard time saying so.

Should Golds need something, they will likely buy it for themselves – or invest in it, as Golds would describe it. If and when Golds ever do borrow anything, returning it immediately becomes priority number one. They believe it is a serious responsibility to be entrusted with someone else's possessions and wish everyone shared that value. When Golds return something they have borrowed, it will be returned in the same condition (or better, cleaner, neater) than how they received it.

What You See and Hear From Golds

Golds tend to wear traditional and conservative attire, and act more formal in their demeanor. They are generally private and reserved, and polite but not gushy. Remember that Golds value a bottom-line approach which will likely be heard in their conversational tone. Golds can also often be identified by their day timers or extensive organizers.

They prefer an organized workspace, and a neat and tidy home. Often there are bulletin boards, and lots of lists, memo pads, or sticky notes. Golds value functionality and practicality – definitely without clutter. Golds also like to have clocks in plain view, or they will frequently look at their watches. Knowing what time it is can be like having a compass for the day.

Golds have a more even and business-like tone of voice and often word things in an either-or, black or white manner. They will ask for specifics and details and are not interested in vague conversations or generalities, all of which can quickly make Golds appear impatient. There will only be basic small talk, just enough to be polite before getting to the point. They will want to know the rules, structure, and the chains of command, and will choose to talk about one subject at a time before moving on.

With an emphasis on short and to-the-point conversations, Golds tend to talk in list form ways, itemizing things as they speak: *"first we should, second, then…"* and so on. It is why they ask mostly closed-ended questions and look for yes or no answers. Since Golds want closure and get things completed, this drive will clearly show in their conversational style.

Now I Understand…

Your strength is measuring success by getting it done. But not just done – done right, done now, and always when you've promised. In the same way, you do things because they need doing – unquestioningly, unwaveringly, and consistently.

I understand how you distinguish between a home and just a house, a job and a career, and doing right versus just doing something. Those are some of the special ways that set you apart from others in your views, attitudes, and values.

You look to be acknowledged for your efforts. So often, your work and help are over and above what anyone could ask. "Like a Rock" really does describe you.

Planning and doing things in good order creates a sense of stability and safety in your future and for those around you.

You are a private person and don't allow everyone into your life. I feel special and honored because you are a true friend, not just a buddy.

You really can't say "no" very often. Your strong sense of duty always shows when you help others and when you give back to your community in many special ways.

No one is harder on themselves than you are – most often needlessly. When it is in moderation, it is the drive that keeps you on-task and focused.

You don't live in the past but keep many special traditions and values alive that provide an invaluable link to the future.

I am your boss or your friend. I am your partner, someone you work with, or your relative... and now I understand you a little better.

Common Gold Strengths

Accurate & detail-oriented

Clear expectations

Conscientious

Considerate & empathetic

Conventional & traditional

Direct & efficient

Family & friends

Giving & helpful

Home is our castle

Loyal

Practical

Punctual

Self-motivated

Sense of accomplishment

Strong willed

Take blame & move on

Thorough

Cautious & traditional

Confident

Conservative

Consistent & dependable

Decisive & in control

Fair and honest

Focused – don't waste time

Great savers

Leaders & great managers

Organized & planning

Predictable

Responsible & reliable

Self-confident

Stable & structured

Supportive & team players

Take charge

Word is our bond

Common Gold Stresses

Acting before plan in place

Being taken advantage of

Clutter & unorganized

Emotions bottled up

Exceptions to rules/vagueness

Getting sidetracked

Hard to trust others

Inefficiency & line-ups

Lack of clear instructions

No loyalty or lack of respect

Not enough time – ever

Others who can't make a decision

People that don't follow through

Reactive & scrambling

Stuck with too much responsibility

Unpredictability

Being late, or anyone who is

Change & lack of routines

Don't like to lose control

Equipment that doesn't work

Feeling overworked

Hard time saying no

Having everyone depend on us

Interruptions

Last minute changes

Non-productive meetings/work

Others deciding priorities

Paranoia over details

Questioning us

Regret taking on too much

Too many things unfinished

Worrying too much

Yeah, feels weird. This is our first night at home in 2 weeks.
It's not right... we've got to do something tonight...

That was a gift from work, since I'm the Queen of
handling challenges and putting out fires.

Chapter Five

Oranges: Freedom and Skillfulness

The drive to enjoy life to the fullest and to multi-task

The focus of: "Just Do It" and "Let's Go!"

Prefer to enjoy the spontaneity of the moment

A classic line: *"Winning isn't everything – it's the only thing!"*

A great quote: *"Hey, I'm just someone who can make quick decisions and think on my feet. I'm sorry you can't."*
Talk show host Charles Adler

I believe that life is a game to be played to win with fun, variety, creativity, and not too much planning or structure. I love competition and interacting with other people. I avoid boredom and routines at almost all cost. I am a natural troubleshooter who doesn't mind rolling up my sleeves and getting involved hands-on and I greatly value my freedom, courage, and high energy level. I'm ready and able to act on a moment's notice – just watch me!

When an Orange comes into our day, we will usually know. He or she is easy to spot with their enthusiastic attitude, sense of humor, and playful nature. Oranges enjoy being noticed and recognized and have no problem becoming the center of attention. They value being unique and showing off, which usually includes the latest, greatest, and coolest stuff. From the clothes they wear to the cars they drive, image is very important, and they act, talk, and dress like winners.

Get To the Point

Communication styles are quite unique for Oranges, which is a challenge for the rest of the world to understand. They love rapid back-and-forth exchanges and immediate answers, results, and feedback. In other words, call them, text them, or catch them, instead of using mail, fax, or e-mail. They want quick answers and decisions, and any delay can bring out their impatient streak.

Oranges are also not above cutting someone off when an answer or explanation starts to drag on. They simply do not need that much information to get going or to make a decision. If others cannot explain something in the length of time it takes to ride an escalator – don't start. While their bottom-line approach can seem rude at times, it is not meant to be. Oranges simply want people to get to the point, keep it positive, make it quick, and tell it like it is – now.

Every Orange does experience the occasional "Orange moment." At times, they really wish they could get the words back into their mouths. Oranges tend to tell it like it is, and sometimes their direct, shoot-from-the-hip comments are difficult for others to handle. Talking or acting before thinking can get them into trouble. But then, their belief is: *"Don't ask me a question if you don't want to hear the answer!"*

A Different Kind of Creativity

Oranges, along with their Blue friends, are very creative. Their process of developing ideas or plans happens by talking things through and perfecting an idea as they go along. Oranges may literally start to talk until they can think of the right thing to say. *"If we want to really promote that, we could get someone to – no, that won't work. What if we all get up and…no, I've got it! We should…"* is the way many Oranges think something through while talking. Should others cut them off half way through this process, they are robbed of the fourth or fifth idea, which is likely to be incredibly brilliant, and something few others would ever have thought of.

With their great creativity, large numbers of Oranges are drawn to construction, mechanical or renovation businesses, or certainly a wide range of other hands-on jobs in which to utilize their great creativity. Others might see only a blueprint, but Oranges can vividly see the finished project. Many people would be turned off by an abandoned, run down old house with shag carpeting and dingy windows, but Oranges visualize the three-dimensional renovated dream home and the incredible potential it holds.

In this type of career, their brain starts going into immediate overdrive. *"We need to tear down this wall, change these windows, dark hardwood floor, light chocolate paint throughout, double the size of the kitchen, take out this bedroom and convert it to a huge walk-in closet...."* all the while becoming seriously excited and impatient to get started. At that point, few doubters will have a chance to stand in their way, or to deter Oranges from their vision.

Restaurant Makeover is a renovation show on the Food Network. One of the episodes featured guest designer Cherie Stinson taking on the renovations of a Toronto restaurant. It was Stinson's Orange versus her two Green restaurant partners. During the first quarter of the show, Stinson attempted to convince both owners that their place was "dingy, dark, 1990 decor, crappy cluttered, and a bar that looked like it was built by a 10-year old." It became apparent that she wanted to (make that: was going to) gut the place, whereas the owners had been looking for a new paint job, at most.

When it comes to creativity and visualizing the renovation process, or envisioning decorating changes, always bet on the

Orange and trust them on this! The same holds true for most high Blues. Designer Sherry Stinson's Orange was not going to cave in, settle, compromise, or make a deal of any kind. She was also the reason this episode had a course language warning – not something that would be necessary with a Blue designer.

What was her solution to the impasse? Agree to "minor changes" and just get the owners to leave for the week. But then, the typical Orange mindset tends to be: I'd rather ask for forgiveness than permission or: Yea – whatever – I'm going to do this and you'll love it when I'm done! (Yes – news flash: they do that at work, too!)

Within a couple of hours, her crew had gutted the entire restaurant. But imagine the look of horror on the face of the owners. "Well," said Stinson, "we might as well keep going now…" which simply had the hyperventilating owners leave again. While she may have had no credibility with the Green owners, the end result was worth it when the comments started with "nice and good" but quickly escalated to "awesome and amazing."

In planning a Christmas party, creating ideas for a team, or holding a church fundraiser, it makes a big difference when any Orange is involved. After all, we cannot be specialists at everything – but this is an area where our Orange friends or teammates excel and really come through. For an Orange, this type of project is not work, but fun, and an awesome challenge. They will win – and we will love it! Like the words of a bumper sticker: *"Sit down, hold on, and shut up."*

Nothing is Set in Stone

Oranges are incredibly flexible and don't get hung up on fixed routines since everything can be negotiated and changed. Their love of competition and the ability to think on their feet makes large numbers of Oranges powerful and successful sales people. A *no* to an Orange is almost always taken as a *maybe*, and simply increases the challenge to use their charm, humor, and skills of persuasion. Assuming they even hear the word *no* – it will be full speed ahead to pursue the sale, or find a way to get what they want. All they need is another approach or a different angle to accomplish their goal and make the deal. Their flexibility and great verbal skills are something Oranges learned as kids when they were able to frequently talk their way out of getting grounded, and a skill they have been fine-tuning ever since.

Yes We Can

Almost all Oranges have a never-ending level of self-confidence and optimism. They intrinsically know that their attitude controls their altitudes and the quality of their lives. Their eternal optimism is not phony or practiced, but an ever-present part of the DNA of their Color. Even in difficult times, Oranges will stay positive and unwavering in their optimism, believing that tomorrow, the next project, or the next client, will always be better. Until then, Oranges will fake it until they make it.

An Orange's winning attitude and a drive to never fail or get down on themselves, creates a powerful mindset. When combined with a commission, plan, recognition, or a dare, Oranges are well on their way to being seriously motivated.

> *"Passion on fire is way better*
> *than knowledge on ice."*
> Shane Rudman

Show Me the Money

Money is certainly a double-edged sword for Oranges. They likely earn lots, and are very generous with their money, but there is just never enough of it. While that mindset applies to most people, it is a different issue for this group. Oranges will tend to make a lot of money, but they will spend it just as quickly. It is rare for Oranges to be concerned with the price of something, anything! Their motto is to rationalize that if it is worth having, just buy it.

In a store or elsewhere in their lives, Oranges make many impulsive decisions. No self-respecting Orange would wander through a mall for hours on end. *Get in, get it, and get out! Find it, like it, buy it – the end.* Money is used to buy toys and cool stuff, and whoever has the most toys wins. And by the way, winning is everything!

No wonder Oranges are motivated by commission pay and bonus plans. These types of pay plans create the freedom to do whatever it takes to control the size of their paycheck. When they run short of money, they will always be able to earn more of it quite quickly. Bonus plans, tips, or commissions, are concrete motivators and scorecards which allow Oranges to live the lifestyle they choose – and be rewarded in direct proportion to their talents and efforts.

Oranges are also very generous with their friends, family, and others when it comes to money. If dividing a $54 tab by three, their impatience will quickly show with something so silly. Their likely response will be, *"here's some money – let's get out of here."*

Releasing Some Energy

The two most common New Year's resolutions are to work out and to get organized. The former does not frequently apply to Oranges. Most have realized long ago, that being physically active acts as an important outlet for their pent-up energy. It is something pretty easy to spot when they start playing with a pen, tapping their feet, shuffling in their chair, getting up, or doodling.

These are the most faithful and active members of fitness clubs. Or, they may enjoy walking, running, mountain biking, softball, or many other team sports. After a week of not doing anything physical, Oranges will admit to become quite fidgety, a little stir-crazy, and ready to explode.

The resolution of getting organized is a challenge of a different kind. Chances are *that* resolution will be on the list again for years to come. Organization is in the eye of the beholder, and Oranges will never buy into the Gold definition of neat piles and labeled boxes. Being organized means they can find what they need, when they need it. Yes, many times Oranges wish they were more organized. But those occasional thoughts are not enough of a priority to make it happen to any significant degree or anytime soon.

Winging It

Oranges are incredible multi-taskers who love to have many things on the go and can juggle a ton of work with ease. Staying crazy-busy creates an adrenalin rush and makes life much more fun. Oranges do not worry about some due-date down the road. It's the right now deadlines which cause them to scramble, get focused, and get it done. They could well be having lunch and suddenly remember a report that is due in an hour. No problem! It will all work out and it is never a reason to panic. Too much preparation is highly over-rated and totally unnecessary. Ulcers are something Oranges might cause, but they are the least likely Color to suffer from them.

Oranges would far prefer to wing it, keep their options open, and see what happens. Thinking on their feet and figuring everything out as they go along is how Oranges function best. They have not wasted a lot of time and energy on needless preparation and this gives them the chance to stay flexible, be open to better ideas, and adapt to changes as they go along. Changing tracks when necessary is never a problem if new or better information comes along.

These traits are something most kids share until their early teens before their personality types fully develop or manifest within themselves. Oranges are just fortunate enough to retain many of these strengths and talents. Not too much planning, thinking on their feet, less worry and more fun, are all traits Oranges will always cherish and defend for a lifetime.

> *"I'm very intuitive, and I jump steps ahead. Part of*
> *what gets me in trouble…is that I shorthand things."*
> Former Presidential Candidate & Governor Howard Dean

Just Do It!

Oranges become successful at anything they set their minds to through hands-on efforts, rather than through practice, theory, textbooks, or manuals. They want to do it, instead of talk about it. The best way to become better at anything in life, happens in real-live situations where the adrenaline is pumping, there is something at stake, and there is a reason to focus and concentrate. Or as Sir Richard Branson describes his business philosophy in his book, *Losing My Virginity*: "Oh, *screw it, let's do it.*"

Any environment which involves the survival of the fittest, and unique situations that require constant flexibility and creativity, are a magnet for Oranges. In the entertainment business, actress Laura

Linney has some great insights into the mindset of Hollywood, and Orange entertainers. After all, Oranges are natural performers no matter what their jobs or ages. Linney describes how typical entertainer's needs and desires to perform, totally outweigh the logical odds of becoming successful. As well, the huge numbers of highs and lows they experience require a very different set of skills and traits. To paraphrase Linney: *You need a certain personality to deal with that lifestyle and the rejection, constant change, and chance of failure, because you can never succeed if you are too self-conscious, or worried about what others may think.*

Those same traits and mindsets apply to the music business where many well-known stars and Orange weekend musicians, have never taken any formal training. Oranges are much more interested (and learn much better) by simply picking up an instrument and seeing what they can do or create. They look to push the boundaries, experiment, and try the impossible without being held back by rules or being told how to do something. That is real freedom; it is the Orange definition of truly living, and not only in the music industry.

> *Without knowing if superstar Bruce Springsteen is Orange, his interview with 60 Minutes had many great Orange insights. Shares Springsteen on behalf of millions of Orange kids: "I was probably one of the smartest kids in my class at the time. You wouldn't have known it. Just because (of) where my intelligence lay I was not able to be tapped in that particular system. I didn't know how to do it myself until music came along and opened me up, not just to the world of music, but to the world period... That engaged me in life and gave me a sense of purpose. What I wanted to do, who I wanted to be, the way I wanted to do it, what I thought I could accomplish..."*

> *Springsteen relates the story of his struggles growing up, and that his father sure was never keen or supportive of his choice*

to become a musician (to put it mildly). "He wasn't very proud of you," stated 60 Minutes co-anchor Scott Pelly. "He was later," responds Springsteen. "When I came home with the Oscar and I put it on the kitchen table he just looked at it and said: 'Bruce, I'll never tell anybody what to do, ever again.'"

As children and adults, Oranges hate being measured for attempts, which only kills their drive to experiment. Results always speak louder than words. Springsteen winning the Oscar, the Orange salesperson landing the big contract after months of negative feedback, or the Orange kid coming through in the class play, victories and successes sure are sweet.

Yes, Oranges will become very successful in a career which interests them, holds their attention, or becomes something they can win at. Until they find their place and reach that point, what are the judgments other Colors have? What do others want to "force" Oranges to do? How much emphasis do parents, coworkers, friends, or bosses place on the process, instead of the results? Are others supportive of the Orange dreams and the impossible goals, or will they be judged through the values and judgments of the other Colors?

The Drive to Win

From sports to sales contests or board games, Oranges want to win. This drive is a large part of their identity. Whoever coined the saying: *"it's not whether you win or lose, its how you play the game,"* wasn't an Orange. It is no wonder vast numbers of them become professional athletes.

> *"Nothing is sweeter than the taste of victory.*
> *Oranges can, and almost always do, make*
> *most things into a contest. It not only*

helps them to focus, but also acts as a
huge motivator and adrenalin rush."

Down by two touchdowns, six runs in softball, eight strokes in golf, or seventh in a sales contest, is just the right time for an Orange to get serious. Others might be packing it up at that point, but Oranges are just getting motivated. Having their backs against the wall may make others crumble, but this becomes an Orange's wake-up call, when they will really start to thrive. When the pressure is on, the whole world has given up, and nobody believes that they can pull it off or come out on top, *that* is the fun that will make their victory that much sweeter. The competition, the drive to win, other like-minded people who won't back down from a challenge, all that media attention, all those fans…yes!

Sure, the money is great, but it is not their primary motivator. More than one pro athlete has said publicly that he plays the games for free; it's the practices he wants to get paid for. Practices, like meetings at work, or too many routines, are neither fun nor productive for Oranges. Out there on the field, in sports, or in business, when everyone is counting on them and watching is where real life happens! Nike's slogan *Just do it* is not just for marketing purposes; but part of the DNA of Oranges. Plus, it's no coincidence that Nike is the name of the Greek goddess of Victory.

"Victory is everything. You can spend the money
but you can never spend the memories."
Ken Venturi

Oranges know that nobody remembers who came in second place. Second is just the first loser, and when it comes to winning, Oranges very much share their Gold friends, black or white mindset. If they believe they cannot be successful, Oranges often choose not to participate in the first place. But once they are committed to a game, a contest, or a project, Oranges will be all business – no sight-seeing, no distractions, no detours, no excuses. Their friendships and teamwork approach will endure, but will have to take a backseat for the time being.

The drive to win can also show itself during discussions or arguments when Oranges do not fight fair – they fight to win. They may bring up something from years ago, dodge or avoid an issue, or not be shy about verbally hitting below the belt. Or, Oranges will use one of their favorite words in the world to end arguments: *"Whatever!"* At that stage, it is best for the other person to understand that they have made their point. To prolong the argument would only make things worse.

A Special Orange Challenge

For years, vast numbers of Oranges have been labeled as rule breakers and trouble makers. Does that make many Oranges just bad actors? Not at all! Many of the rules created by a "Gold" society do not fit the Orange's style or personality. Oranges typically challenge boundaries and the status quo. They do have a strong value system, but it can be uniquely theirs. Some were either never taught, or are currently not interested, in conforming to what the world considers appropriate behaviors.

On the other side of the coin are huge numbers of extremely successful Oranges – vast numbers of whom are highly successful managers, CEOs, and the largest group of entrepreneurs. The Oranges who conform within the basic rules and norms of society have not lost their fight for freedom or uniqueness at all. When their energies, talents, and drive to win are channeled in positive directions, they generally become very powerful and often unstoppable.

Hurry Up

From cars to motorcycles, conversations to sports, our Orange friends love speed, action, and everything fast. Other Colors will have a hard time keeping up, but do not look for Oranges to slow down, either. They have a never-ending drive for adventure, and will always be energetic and optimistic.

Even decisions come quickly as Oranges simply do not have the time to linger over most questions and issues. Conversations quickly jump from one topic to another. To keep up, others need to stay flexible and on their toes. When Oranges call to do something, they are likely already in their car and on their way. Seldom will anyone have much notice to decide whether they want to come along. If it takes too long to decide – no problem, they are going without them. Their loss.

"I was retired for 12 hours. Eight of those I slept
and then I wanted to start a new business."
Buddy – owner of Finn McCool Restaurant

In retail sales, few things are more hilarious than watching sales people totally unable to speed up, or to switch gears when targeting presentations to Orange customers. Slow sales people, too much paperwork or hassle, will have Oranges leaving empty handed. In fact, studies have shown that more than $20 billion in merchandise is left at checkout counters each year as customer walk out of stores. It would not be much of a stretch to assume the majority of these lost sales are from Orange customers who refuse to be stuck in a line-up.

ADD? Not Likely

Attention Deficit Disorder (ADD) is something plenty of Oranges have been asked about, or labeled as, at some point or another. In fact, drug makers now claim that over eight million adults "suffer" from ADD in North America. Maybe. Without downplaying the legitimacy of ADD, there are many more millions of Oranges who laugh at that label and know fully well that many so-called "symptoms" are their normal stresses and behaviors.

The web-site of one drug maker even claims that a simple six-question quiz establishes whether someone is likely to have symptoms of ADD. Their assessment ranges from whether the person has trouble finishing projects, has difficulty sitting still for long periods without fidgeting, challenges with getting started on detailed projects, or has trouble planning tasks in order. There are very few Oranges who would not be able to answer yes to all of those questions, or they wouldn't be Orange! It is no wonder this drug maker's marketing resulted in more than one million prescription sales in just the first six months on the market.

Are these really "problems," or just special gifts and talents? Finishing details is a last-minute thing. Right now, Oranges choose to multi-task as there are lots of others things on their plate. Sitting still is not always a challenge, but it does depend on whether a meeting or project is interesting, interactive, or practical in the first place. Getting tasks in order is not half as much fun as working on pieces here and there, a little bit at a time. That approach simply creates variety and avoids boredom – it does not create a need for drugs. Oranges will get their work done, but it is going to be a lot of fun along the way. It just may not be done with the same template the rest of the world is using.

Oranges have the ability to multi-task with ease, and with little or no stress. They have the drive to be challenged. If that comes with some impulsiveness, distraction, and avoiding paperwork, would many people not take that trade-off? In the words of former JetBlue founder David Neeleman during a 60 Minutes feature on adult ADD:

"Your brain just thinks a little different and you come up with things. I just have a feeling that if I took the medication, I'd be just like everybody else."

Many critics are even harsher, describing much of the two billion dollar ADD industry as marketing lifestyle drugs. While the truth is likely somewhere in the middle, the tools and insights of Colors certainly play a large role in understanding Oranges and their great strengths, skills, and outlook on life.

> *Thank heavens for my understanding Colors, or I would have been making a huge mistake with my Orange daughter. She does drive me crazy with ten things on the go. But, instead of yelling at her, and making things worse, I have learned unbelievable patience and gentle nudging. Believe it or not, it works! It is hard to resist the urge to become judgmental, jump in, or hurry her along. But an understanding of how Oranges think and act helps our family, strengthens our relationship, and will equip her for a lifetime of success and not medication.* – C.G.

Friends and Buddies

Oranges love to be around people and are very approachable and friendly. Their easy-going and fun attitude, great sense of humor and social nature, make them great friends and fun to be around. Oranges have a natural gift of making anyone and everyone feel like they are best friends already. This large circle of friends and an incredible array of contacts is also their extensive networking group. Should someone need to connect with a business, get a referral, find a new employee, or look for a cool restaurant, Oranges are the go-to people. They will know somebody, or they will always know somebody who knows somebody…

The Heck with What They Think

Without the insights of Colors, many people wonder about their Orange friends, family members, or fellow employees. When will they grow up, act more responsibly, get more serious, get better organized, or "come around" in some way or another? The answer is: *Never.* Or in the words of a very Orange-descriptive song by Mindy McCready: *"Well, I pay a price being independent…This is me, take it or leave it. What you see is what I am and who I want to be – this is me!"*

It was actually her grandson who brought Karen to the seminar. It was just after her 75th birthday, and somehow her grandson had enough insight to know that she would get lots of value from understanding Colors.

For the first part, she sat quietly, smiled a lot, and just listened. But when the Color groups were separated, Karen quickly joined the Oranges. She was and is a high Orange! The last ten years in a nursing home hadn't changed her at all but had certainly created a mask. A mask that was perhaps meant to hide who she really was, but after all those years it had actually started to define her, instead.

Age had not changed Karen's personality. It had simply mellowed her, reduced her volume control, and her physical energy was certainly a lot less in comparison to a 20-something Orange. But she still bugged people all the time to play cribbage, cards, or some kind of game where she could have some competition and the chance to win. She was friends with everyone in the nursing home and the staff loved her.

At the end of the seminar she shared with me: "I'm back! And I'm gonna buy a canoe! I've always wanted to have a canoe to be out on the lake and to have freedom to go wherever I want and whenever I want. I'm going to do it!"

I don't know if Karen ever did buy that canoe. It was never about the canoe anyway, but about seeing the sparkle in her eyes that morning and about an Orange person finding the words and explanations to understand who she really is. Perhaps it was giving herself permission to be who she really was and is, and to put away the mask of conformity.

What You See and Hear From Oranges

It is always easy to spot a high Orange. They like to dress trendy and love the latest fashions, and the coolest, greatest gadgets. Their workspace can be quite messy and they may have some sports equipment lying nearby. They also tend to misplace things. Oranges have an active and confident demeanor. A real challenge for them is sitting still for extended time periods, as they exhibit lots of fidgeting, quick movements, and gestures, and may well show their impatience. If Oranges have pictures on the wall, they love including some of themselves involved with famous people, receiving an award, or attending a sporting event.

When you listen to an Orange, you can sense that same high energy level. Even in the more quiet places like their church, it is usually easy to notice when a group of Oranges arrive, as the volume level will certainly increase. They love laughter and humor, and will quickly jump from subject to subject, talking quite fast, with a high energy level, and an animated voice. They are natural name-droppers and use it to connect with others. After all, if we both know so and so, we are practically friends already! Oranges are perpetual networkers, so they often promote ideas or businesses. They often ask probing and direct questions. They value discussing big picture stuff without getting bogged down with too many specifics or details. Keep conversations to the point, stay flexible, and bring your sense of humor.

Now I Understand…

I recognize that being on time is often a challenge and may be more important to me than to you. The clock should not measure the value of our relationship anyway.

I value and look for your high energy that makes you a magnet to others who seek you out. I can't duplicate it, but I also gain energy from being around you.

Sometimes my role is just to finish up something or pick up the pieces. Yes, I may grumble or complain, but I also know if it weren't for you, we probably wouldn't have gotten started at all.

You teach me not to be too serious about many situations. I continue to learn that it is ok to laugh at myself. You pull me out of my shell, sometimes fighting or resisting – but don't give up.

You teach in ways others don't – not through textbooks or talking about it. You do it by example, by rolling up your sleeves and actually doing it.

Your ability to change tracks and your "let's go" attitude is something I value learning from you. Sometimes I may not participate, but just love watching you in action. With you there is seldom a dull moment.

Few others have your combination of talent and personality. You value freedom as much as others value knowing you. I was a lot more like you as a kid. Watching you, I sometimes wonder how the world has closed in on me, where you have managed to keep so much of your free spirit.

I am your boss or your friend. I am your partner, someone you work with or your relative… and now I understand you a little better.

Common Orange Strengths

Active

Adventurous

Artistic

Awesome sales people

Direct

Don't get stressed

Energizer bunnies

Entertaining & fun

Fast paced

Flexible

Freedom

Generous

Great sense of humor

Great with tools – hands on

Having fun

Impatient

Impulsive

Just do it!

Life is never boring

Love attention

Low stress

Loyal & caring

Open-minded

Optimistic

Outrageous & vocal

People magnet

Ready & able to change

Risk-takers

Skillful

Social

Spontaneous

Unpredictable

Winging it

Winning – always

Common Orange Stresses

Boredom & lack of action

Chained to a desk

Challenge to finish stuff

Conformity

Fixed rules & policies

Hate to lose

Having to be on time

How-to manuals

Lack of choices

Losing things

Making lists

Manuals & procedures

Meetings & deadlines

Needy people

Non-party people

Not enough challenges

Not enough recognition

Not enough money

Paperwork

Political correctness

Rigid schedules

Routines

Sappy songs

Sitting still

Slow people

Sore losers

Structure & rules

Whiners, complainers & worriers

No, when they said you had a "Green face"
they weren't talking about anything medical.

I agree we want the perfect computer system.
But it's our first anniversary, we should really get it soon...

Chapter Six

Greens: Knowledge and Understanding

The drive to gather the facts and research all options
before making a decision

The focus on a lifetime of learning and exploring

Seek to examine all experiences so they can be
improved next time

A classic line: *"Sarcasm is humor, too"*

A great quote: *"Speak from the heart? A heart is an organ. It pumps
and circulates blood, it doesn't, however, speak!"*
Christina – Grey's Anatomy

*I believe in remaining calm, cool, and collected in any situation.
I value knowledge and learning and enjoy passing that knowledge on to others who want to learn. I am intelligent and logical
and can be a perfectionist. I am analytical and enjoy thinking
things through. I want to explore all possibilities and avenues in
my creative and inventive ways before committing myself or
making a decision. I prefer to look at the big picture and can
consistently be counted on to provide accurate and logical
information and answers.*

Greens live in a world of facts and logic, which is quite different
from Blues who function through intuition and feelings. Greens are
leaders and not followers. They have a sharp mind and never-ending
desire to grow – questioning the status-quo, and pursuing a lifetime

of learning. Consequently, Greens are often a number of steps ahead of others in their plans, ideas, and visions.

The Green mindset greatly values knowledge and understanding. They thrive on constant mental challenges because they have really never met a juicy problem they did not want to tackle. They believe curiosity takes courage. Greens create and look for logic and competence, not only in processes, but in the people they work with, and in the framework or structure of their environment. These are the trend-setters and visionaries, never the "yes" people or the followers. Wondering what others are doing, or conforming to the norm is of little interest to Greens. They were strong-willed and independent as six-year olds, and will be for a lifetime.

Information is Power

From their childhood to retirement, Greens love to learn. It is a life-long hobby and a drive, which makes them very knowledgeable and above average, intellectually. Greens are on a constant search for understanding anything and everything of interest to them. Since the Green mind is constantly processing and analyzing everything they encounter, information truly is power.

> *"Strange how much you've got to know*
> *before you know how little you know."*
> Author Unknown

Questioning how something works, why procedures are in place, or finding improved tools, technology, and processes are some of their special strengths. Greens prefer to focus on big picture questions and complex problems. They become annoyed and frustrated when they are unable to access credible information, or when current procedures or methods are no longer efficient or logical. Greens cannot conceive how anyone would settle for sub-par procedures or operating methods when there are clearly better ways. Greens might not give in, but they sure would not give up, either.

Greens are constantly thinking about one thing or another. Even in the line-up at a retailer, they will be evaluating the store's inefficiencies and wondering what kind of dummies designed these stores. The downside is that there is never a pause button for their mind. Most Greens admit that there are nights when it can take hours to fall asleep, simply because they cannot shut down their thought processes. Those nights, Greens often turn on their iPod, or the television with the sleep timer, to allow their mind to focus on something mundane in order to relax and find their off switch.

Greens are continuously driven to learn and grow and look for complete and accurate factual feedback and answers to their "why" and "how" questions. So imagine their motivation when it comes to their own life and death decisions:

> The Patient from Hell *is not only the title of a book by Professor Stephen Schneider, but probably also how many medical professionals might describe Greens. Should they become seriously ill, Greens will usually start their own treatment with a mindset of wanting to, and needing to, learn as much as they can, and begin to understand everything that may be involved.*

> *This included a lot of research on the web, in spite of being told not to bother because it would just depress and confuse him. Wrong! Schneider, like every Green, believes a large factor in his being alive today was his persistence and willingness to ask questions, unlike most patients he describes as believing their role to be taking orders and staying co-operative. From talking a surgeon out of his scheduled biopsy surgery, to the simple use of a needle, to changes in medication through persistent questions*

and explored alternatives, he challenged specialists and unearthed critical information for his own treatment. Schneider is now in remission, something he fully credits to taking charge of his own destiny.

Dealing with Hurt and Emotions

When Greens are hurt, they care and feel just as deeply as every other Color. It is just not something that manifests itself with a lot of external clues, or anything they are comfortable sharing with other people. When they are hurting, Greens prefer to be alone, unplug the telephone, tune out the world, and likely turn on (or turn to) their computer, iPad, or other tech gadgets.

It is quite uncomfortable, and very unusual, for Greens to show their feelings in public. They do not believe they will somehow feel better by talking it through. If Greens do choose to discuss their feelings or frustrations, it will be more in the way of a debriefing and will likely be with another Green who will assure the conversation stays logical and rational. As the above story of Stephen Schneider describes so well, there is really nothing which cannot be healed or solved with sufficient research, information, and alone time.

In all of their relationships, emotional outbursts, like public displays of affection, are quite rare with Greens. Verbal affirmations for their staff, or holding hands with their partner, are learned traits, but still a little out of a Green's comfort zone. Yes, someone is doing a good job, and they certainly do love their partner, but it is not something that needs to be repeated day after day.

Mother's day note: My Mother's day was the same as any other. That's the norm for Mother's day, our anniversary, Christmas, and my birthday. I have to celebrate on my own.

Next day note: Just wanted to clarify my note from yesterday.
I wanted to add that I love my husband, and he loves me, but
gift giver and celebrator he is not. I have learned to value that he
shows me love in other ways.   – A.K.P.

Bluff Me and I'm Gone

The primary core value for Greens is their need for credibility. Any business, sales person, or even coworker who bluffs their way through a question or lies to a Green, is dead – period. Greens will leave and will never ever return. It is perfectly OK to tell any Green person that you do not have the answer. Just get back to them with the information, preferably by e-mail – with correct spelling, proper grammar, and always when promised. Most Greens will also admit that their drive for credibility includes family and friends who do not have some special exemption.

Trial lawyers believe that one should never ask a question without knowing the answer. Greens often practice this approach as well. In a meeting, at a store, or with a staff member, they can often ask one or two questions where they already know the answers. Why? It is simply to test the credibility of the other person.

Green Time

The generally accepted definition of organization comes from Golds and consists of neat piles, a clean desk, and labeled file folders. Yet, the word organization, like the definition of family, honesty, or fun has four very different definitions for each Color. If Greens are asked to choose between being physically organized, or "thoughts organized," almost every one of them will pick the definition of being mentally organized.

It is why every Green needs to have a certain amount of "alone," or Green time each day. For this half hour to an hour, they need to be alone to think things through, process information, figure something out, plan their strategies, or work through some problem or another.

While others, including their partners, can misinterpret this as anti-social behavior, or that perhaps a Green is mad at them, nothing could be further from the truth. This independent processing and thinking time is invaluable and mandatory. It might involve working on some project in the garage, taking up a solo sport such as running, or often just having some time on the computer or reading. However, their Green time is not just about being active in doing something. It also creates the time for Greens to simply unwind or reflect on the flaws, stupidity, and imperfections of the world.

Even at parties and social functions, Greens generally start to drift to the sidelines after an hour or two. They may be enjoying themselves just as much as anyone else, but only for limited periods of time before their energy levels start to drain. Nothing is wrong, they simply choose not to stay in the middle of the action and noise, and are quite content in people-watching from the sidelines. Besides, other Greens have likely taken the same approach, and they may meet another Green with whom they are able to strike up a great discussion.

Recently, our family hosted the current reigning World Junior Champions in their sport for a tournament against the Chinese National Team, here to train for the Olympics.

After breakfast, Chris, the captain, got up from the table and sat outside in his car, all alone, without a word to anyone. As I sat staring out the window at him wondering what was wrong, one of the other boys came up to me and said, "Don't take it personal. Chris just gets moody. We've learned to just ignore him when he's like that." And after about 20 minutes sitting in the car,

Chris just drove off alone, leaving the rest of the team to pack up all the equipment and arrange their own transportation.

Later that evening, they spotted the Colorful Personalities book. Chris immediately took the quiz, and as he read the characteristics of Greens he had just a hint of a grin. And this is most unusual for Chris, as they call him "poker face," because his face remains the same, whether his dog just died, or he's won the lottery. When his teammates did the assessment, he bluntly challenged one of them for not being honest. It was something his teammate admitted, as he was afraid the others would think he was too soft. To which Chris replied: "But every team needs a Blue!" He couldn't have paid his teammate a higher compliment!

The next morning, Chris again snuck off to the car for his alone time, but his team now laughed and commented: "That's our Green Chris." But today it was said with pride, respect and admiration for their captain as Chris prepared for the next game in his own unique ways. What was perceived one day as moody, selfish, and rude, became a source of respect. The behavior did not change – just the perception and understanding. These are 20 year old world-class athletes with an amazing amount of pressure to retain their World title and coached by some of the best technical advisors in the world. Yet they learned way more from the tools of Colors about themselves, each other, and the values and strengths of their Green captain. – S.K. (The names have been changed and the sport omitted. Yes, they did go on to repeat as National Champions.)

What You See Is Not What You Get

Talking with most Greens takes some special skills and a confident mindset. With their neutral facial expression, others can question if Greens are really listening. This is especially challenging for the people-first Blues and Oranges. Oranges are very visual and look for feedback to take any conversations or presentations from there. But with Greens, there is very little to see. Blues have an even harder time. With their animated expressions, Blues mirror any conversation through their facial expressions. Talking with Greens can have Blues wondering whether they are talking too much (for Greens, they are) or whether the Green person is really listening.

None of these feelings and questions are true or accurate. Yes, Greens are listening. In fact, they are some of the best listeners – as long as they believe there is value in the conversation or presentation and someone can be brief, be bright, and be gone. Greens are absorbing the information, evaluating every comment, and thinking through the implications. Their mental computer is on, and their notebook is open. They simply do not value interactive banter and prefer to just sit and listen without interrupting.

Greens are not scary, mad, or cold, and it is entirely inaccurate to judge them based on their calm and cool demeanor or their neutral expression. Their lack of a "friendly face" is almost always interpreted inaccurately. From Stephen Harper who was continuously labeled as having a "hidden agenda" by opposition parties, to Hillary Clinton's frequent description as cold and uncaring, Greens are continuously mischaracterized simply because of their lack of facial expressions.

What people should know about me: "Most people
take my look as being mad. I'm not – it's just a look."
Profile write-up on a dating web site

Communicating with Greens is best done by focusing conversations on logic and facts. They prefer discussions that are well articulated, concise, and to the point. Feeling-based talk, excessive kidding around, redundant questions, or hyping up a conversation can quickly have Greens out of their comfort zone and tuned out.

Conversations and discussions are more like a tennis match. The ball is in the other court, now they talk. After that, there will be a couple of seconds delay while Greens process the information, think ahead to what is really being asked, and respond with few words that are well thought out. Greens also respond to many questions with another question. With their large vocabulary and depth of knowledge, Greens can certainly seem intimidating to others.

Getting respect from Greens is something to be earned and is never given away freely. Greens are never accused of being people pleasers or of going along with something just to get along with anyone. They have a lot more respect for others who will stand up for themselves and show courage in their convictions. Confrontation is not confrontation or conflict at all if someone brings the facts, knows their stuff, has done their homework, and can articulate their case. Any of those will get the attention of Greens and create respect and credibility. All the while, the Green person will be wondering what took them so long...

*"You people are telling me what you think I want to know.
I want to know what is actually happening."*
Creighton Abrams

Just Say No

Greens strive to make proper and correct decisions that are well thought out, accurate, and justifiable. When they are pressed for immediate answers, Greens will likely reply with a simple and direct *"no."* What this answer actually translates to is: *"if you want an answer right now before I can think about it, the answer is no – now go away."*

Important questions with large implications require time to formulate a correct answer. Pushing Greens to come up with complex solutions off the top of their heads will not elicit a response. Honoring Greens through building in some thinking-time will result in well-informed feedback and decision-making. This approach also elicits a more frequent positive response, instead of a defensive *no* answer just to get someone off their case, or out of their office.

This same mindset applies during meetings where Greens detest decisions made without proper thought or adequate time to research options and alternatives. It is not about making a quick decision – it is about making the right decision. From staff meetings to planning their holidays, Greens need to have access to all information and facts well in advance. It simply allows Greens to be well prepared, ask relevant questions, and contribute their input in meaningful ways. Feedback or ideas will not be forthcoming until they are able to justify their ideas with facts.

Greens are not people who will shoot from the hip or talk without thinking. It will not happen. Their thought process occurs in a logical manner and you can be sure all opinions and options are solidly researched and defendable. At that point, their decision will stand until additional or better information is available which justifies re-visiting the issue.

"Not to know is bad;
not to wish to know is worse."
African Proverb

Pressure and Hype Equals Failure

It is not possible to sell something, anything, to a Green. But selling is not only about selling a product or service since each of us sells many times a day. We attempt to bring others around to our point of view, convince someone of an idea, persuade our partner where to go on vacation, or prove to the kids the value of doing homework.

In the world of sales, Greens do all of their research in advance. They would much rather be online than in line. When they do make a trip to the store it is only to obtain information they have not otherwise been able to get on the Internet. Greens then use the sales staff as their suppliers of missing information. To succeed with Green customers, as with a Green boss, friend, or coworker, sales people need to stay credible and well informed.

Even retailers have now identified Green shoppers. Well, they are not really shoppers, but rather investigators. Research trips focus on separating hype from reality. They avoid salespeople who have little credibility, and whose information is obviously biased and likely inaccurate. The New York based trend-watching firm Euro RSCG Worldwide has even given Greens a name, calling them prosumers. An Ottawa Citizen article describes them as people who diagnose themselves with the help of the Internet before walking into the doctor's office with their research on treatment options. *"Of course,"* would be the Green response. However, retailers still have not learned how to deal with Greens, or understand that major purchases or critical decisions can well take a few months or more. (For more sales insights, see: *The Colors of Sales and Customers*.)

The Drive for Perfection

Greens travel on a lifelong journey to improve procedures and processes. They are well aware that perfection is a constantly moving target, which also becomes a continuous conundrum. It is not necessarily about reaching perfection, but always about moving in that direction. Greens are often quite a bit ahead of their time and see the world in very different ways. They believe that reality really can be altered, and continually challenge others to keep growing, and to work towards how the world could be, rather than simply settling for what it is. This certainly makes them a powerful influence on others, and more often than not, the go-to people for problem solving and innovative solutions.

It is frustrating for Greens to suggest improvements when others won't listen or accept their feedback. Substandard results, the phrase "good enough," or obvious errors and flaws drive Greens nuts, kill credibility, and are a sure-fire way to get their backs up.

Anyone with Internet access is familiar with Wikipedia, the huge on-line, free content encyclopedia with over 17 million entries. The idea was formed in 2001 by two friends as a site where everyone in the world could contribute articles, features and information in an open and unrestricted forum.

One of the original founders of Wikipedia was Larry Sanger. But after only two years, Sanger left the company because he no longer believed in the credibility of Wikipedia when he started to question the accuracy and integrity of many entries and contributions. He walked away after disagreements with his partner as to who should be allowed to contribute to the site, even before it became the giant it is today. As if to prove the point, co-founder Jimmy Wales has edited his own bio, deleting any mention of Sanger's role. It was never about money, fame or success. It is always about credibility and doing it right.

In the words of Sanger himself: "Wikipedia began as a good-natured anarchy, a sort of Rousseauian state of digital nature. I always took Wikipedia's anarchy to be provisional and purely for purposes of determining what the best rules and the nature of its authority should be. What I, and other Wikipedians, failed to realize is that our initial anarchy would be taken by the next wave of contributors as the very essence of the project – how Wikipedia was "meant" to be."

What did the Green Sanger do? He developed a better and more credible site and launched citizendium.org. This site has firm editorial rules and mandatory disclosure of the real names of its editors, whereas Wikipedia allows anyone with a fictitious user name to contribute untraceable content.

Paying it Forward

Should you get sick, do not look for your Green friends to sit by your hospital bed for hours. It won't happen. But you can bet they will bring some magazines, a good book, or a useful article from webmd.com. Why? Because you're sick and should at least utilize this time to read a good book, stimulate your mind, or learn something – anything.

With their lifelong love of learning, payday for Greens is the opportunity to teach and to train others. Of course, that is contingent on someone actually wanting to learn in the first place. Or as Greens would describe it: *You can't water a rock*. Being able to watch others put their knowledge into practice is a powerful way Greens grow their self-esteem. Teaching others is the most tangible way Greens show the world that they really care deeply. Unfortunately, their methods and style are often misunderstood, and can go unnoticed by other Colors. What Greens seldom do, however, is "dummy down" their teaching style (that is how they see it), or simplify many explanations:

Before doing a report cover, Gina e-mailed a friend for some graphics work and a question of whether the report sub-title should have a comma inserted. But for her Green friend, the e-mail was not a simple question about a comma. It was an opportunity to teach Gina its correct use:

"AIUI a non-defining relative clause introduced by "which" should be set off with a comma. Without it, it will be read as

a defining clause (in which "that" would be preferable as the relative pronoun). But I don't think this is what you want to imply here, my evidence being your choices to use the definite article and to capitalize the word…in my opinion, the last bit has a bit more of a problem than can be fixed by a comma, being what might be called a failed parallelism."

Green Discussions and Feedback

To Greens, small talk or idle-chit chat has a lifespan of less than a minute. But for anyone who values an intricate or deep discussion, the chance for a good debate, or to be mentally challenged, Greens are always ready, willing, and more than able to participate. What can intimidate others are their sharp minds and direct or blunt questions. Rather than being intimidated, other Colors need to understand the Green approach as a compliment.

Greens only seriously pursue any discussion or debate with someone whom they judge as having credibility. After all, what's the point of a debate when the other person does not have the knowledge or anything valuable to contribute? Conversely, it is a great compliment when Greens do want to get into a good debate or discussion, because they are judging that person as someone from whom they can learn something and who will challenge their mind.

It is important to remember and to believe that Green feedback is not criticism. When any Green person corrects someone, comments, or points out errors, it is always from a mindset of giving better information. They are not looking for ways to shoot down ideas or to find fault. It is entirely about caring enough to help others to learn, and to do better. Or in the words of Supreme Court Justice Antonin Scalia, *"I attack ideas, I don't attack people."* To Greens, it is more important to be respected than liked, and more valuable to be knowledgeable than popular. Could Greens correct someone a little softer, or less direct? Probably. But the approach should never take away from their intent of caring enough to help.

"My job is not to be easy on people. My job is to take these great people we have and to push them and make them even better… just by coming up with more aggressive visions."
Steve Jobs, Apple CEO

What You See and Hear From Greens

You generally first spot Greens by their calm, cool, and collected demeanor, or their neutral poker-face. If you have ever watched the television show CSI, you have seen many Greens in action (although most Greens find little credibility in the show itself). Often others can feel as though they are being evaluated by Greens, who seldom show visible emotions and can seem reserved or somewhat distant. What to wear is not of great importance, as clothing is a necessity and not usually worn to impress anyone. With most Greens, you will see them with some of the latest gadgets or computers. Their workspace or desk can also be quite messy with the many projects they are perfecting, and you will likely see a lot of books, magazines, or manuals.

When you are listening to a Green, you will hear many "why" and "how" questions. They can show their annoyance at being asked to repeat themselves and will give logical, direct, and specific answers. Greens are people of few words, but their words will be well chosen and with a large vocabulary. Depending on the complexity of an issue, Greens may take a few seconds before answering. Their response may not be instant, but it will always be accurate. They use clever humor or sarcasm and express themselves in terms of "I think," or "I believe," which are logic-type phrases, instead of the Blue "I feel" expressions.

Now I Understand...

Your need for Green time each day is not about me. It is not about being anti-social. It is time you reserve, and need, just for yourself.

Before I press you for an instant response, I should decide if I really need an answer now, or whether I value your well thought out responses.

You think things through properly and do nothing half-way. You look at the big picture and weigh all the options and possibilities. You take the time to see the whole puzzle while I may just be seeing a box of pieces.

With your easy-going nature, your feelings do run deeply. Just because they do not always come to the surface does not mean they are not real or do not exist.

I appreciate spending time with you, and it is not only about talking all the time. Sometimes the best communication with you is when you say nothing at all – just displaying your calm strength, logic, and demeanor.

Your Green face is not a way to measure your listening skills, or a scale to judge how much you care. Behind it is a great amount of caring and an ability to listen to me.

When you ask me a lot of questions, it is not a criticism of what I've said, but rather your never-ending desire to know more and more. It should not a reason for me to become defensive, but an honor that you value learning something from me.

I am your boss or your friend. I am your partner, someone you work with or your relative... and now I understand you a little better.

Common Green Strengths

Analytical & logical

Enjoy our own company

Focus on important things

Great problem solvers

Independent & self-directed

Innovative

Knowing the questions to ask

Learning & teaching others

No question we won't tackle

Perfectionists & high standards

Problem solvers

Self-confident

Skeptical

Theoretical

Visionaries

Credibility

Enjoys solitude

Future oriented

Honest & direct

Ingenuity

Inquisitive

Knowledgeable

Logical & factual

Not overly emotional

Power to ask "what if?"

Rational

Sense of humor

Take nothing for granted

To the point & direct

Well-read/diverse interests

Common Green Stresses

Anticipate problems

Emotional outbursts

Incompetence – self & others

Insufficient information

Intrusion into our comfort zone

Meetings with no point

Not knowing or understanding

Others bluffing us

People in the way of strategy

Quick decisions

Rules that don't make sense

Unfairness & injustice

Deadlines

Forgetting something

Inconsistencies & redundancy

Interruptions

Know we're right & others
who don't believe us

No challenge/too much
repetition & routine

Not enough alone-time

Others who don't value learning

Pushy sales people

Relying on thought process
of others

Spelling & grammatical errors

Chapter Seven

Our Combinations of Colors

Life would sure be easier if all of us were just one personality type. That might give us a simple black and white understanding of the world, but it would also make us quite boring and one-dimensional.

Fortunately, nobody lives only in their primary Color. Each of us functions in many different ways, at different times and circumstances, in all of our four Colors. For many of us, just the way we *need* to act at work may be quite different from how we *choose* to act at home.

The military, for example, is a very Gold culture. All four Colors choose to serve in a variety of areas and for very different reasons and motivators. But all of them have joined a very Gold institution. Following rules, obeying orders, adhering to strict discipline and the chain of command, are not optional when lives depend on it – period. Yet, if a Sergeant comes home and starts to bark out orders to his spouse, or demands a room inspection from the kids, he will face far more combat than he can handle.

There is always a time and a place for every action and every Color. We all know when to have fun and play, or when it is critical to stop the world and think through an important decision with long-term consequences. Everyone certainly recognizes the time to be organized or to have a fixed plan, and would never hesitate to drop everything for a close friend who needs help.

Those two sentences describe the values of all four Colors and every person on earth agrees with each of those points. But there is a time and a place for everything, since our first Color sets our priorities and shapes how we see the world and how we would like it to function. After all, the higher the score of your first Color, the more you will relate to that specific chapter, almost as though it was written just for you. Yet, someone with a closer score between their first two Colors will pick and choose many descriptors from those two sections.

No Color or combination of Colors is better than another. However, they are certainly very different and influence our thoughts, behaviors, strengths, stresses, and values in a wide variety of ways. What makes every person unique is our combination. Just like a jigsaw puzzle, we have all four pieces working together within us. For each of us, this four-Color puzzle comes in a wide variety of shapes and sizes which forms our diversity, strengths, and preferences.

Our second Color plays a significant roll in many behaviors and actions, values, and stresses. It is called our shadow Color; the part of our personality which lies in the shadow of the primary's motivators and strengths. This second Color will always have a strong influence on our values and behaviors.

Our Blue second Color will always remind us to be more patient and caring, and our Orange influence will keep us mindful that it is also OK to just have fun and not take everything too seriously, which can become our anti-stress defense. If our second Color is Green, it is a lifelong reminder to think things through and do something right the first time, while our Gold influence is that voice which insists that we stay focused, structured, and on-time.

Curt is a Blue/Gold Pastor. His first jobs after graduation were in the construction industry. The one thing that always horrified Curt was any project that did not have a complete set of blueprints. His high Gold and very low Orange did not want to just wing it, but needed clear and specific instructions. Long before he had ever heard of Colors, Curt always felt a drive to pursue a more people-oriented career. As a strong Christian, he soon realized his true calling was to be a Pastor.

The years at seminary were both richly rewarding and painfully difficult. His Blue intuition and faith instinctively knew that this was his true purpose in life. Likewise, his high Gold had made a plan and the thought of quitting before graduating was never an option. He had given his word and would see it through no matter what it took.

When Curt received his calling to a congregation, his primary job description was leading the various youth groups and taking charge of the Sunday school. With his natural Gold planning and organizational skills, he was always prepared. From candy to activities, from stories to fun and games, the kids and their parents adored him. While Curt's Blue loved working with people, the talents needed for high Orange kids were quite different than those required in working with adults. His strong core strengths of duty and serving conflicted with his desire to grow and to work in a lesser Orange area of the church.

Today Curt is Dean of Residence to over two hundred students at a very large Bible College. For Curt, it was a dream come true and finally a position which fully utilized the gifts and strengths of his Blue/Gold.

Colors continuously combine to make a multitude of decisions, actions, thoughts, and even set priorities. To the degree which one or the other dominates, depends on the strength (score) of the shadow Color and the importance of one's specific actions or decisions. A Gold/Green will often limit their research for more information in order to get something finished and off their to-do list. The Green shadow Color would love to take the time to make the perfect decision, but the Gold drive for closure sets a time-limit.

For an Orange/Blue person, their need for competition and winning is ever-present. However, the strong Blue people-first influence will draw a line at bragging too much about the win. A Blue second Color will also tend to resist a team sport where others could get hurt, which simply honors a strong Blue value.

> *Our primary and shadow Colors can either complement*
> *each other or clash between two different values.*
> *Whether consciously or not, these battles create*
> *and shape our values in many different ways.*

Our Different View of Others

Through the eyes or glasses of our Colors, we see many situations, and even other people, in very different ways. Just a simple staff meeting is not really simple. For Golds, the drive is more about getting through the agenda in a disciplined manner and finishing on time. Oranges hope to get out of there in less than 15 minutes. *PLEASE! Get to the point, make the decisions, and move on because we have real work to do.* Blues want to ensure that everyone gets a chance to feel included and heard, while Greens value some intelligent discussions, the information in advance, and the chance to think things through properly. Even an every-day event, such as a traffic tie-up can have our four Colors thinking in very different ways:

> *I was sitting in traffic as my 30 Gold score was impatiently waiting to get past an accident. At that point, my high Green started to wonder about the other drivers around me, and how their Colors determined what to do.*
>
> *The Golds were likely in the lane furthest away from the wreck, because you're supposed to move away from an accident, and they were in the lane they needed to be in, planning to make their exit a long ways ahead. They were*

irritated that some people weren't moving to the open lane since there was a sign way ahead of the tie-up warning everyone that there was an accident in the far left lane!

The Blues were probably in the next lane over so that they could help people move over away from the accident, but also in order to help people get on and off the exits. They were also in this lane so they would see the wreck to make sure no one was hurt or needed help. They had already dialed 911 on their cell and were waiting to press the "send" button in case help was needed. Perhaps the Greens were in the lane next to the accident in order to evaluate how many cars were in the wreck, how it happened and whose fault it was – all in an effort to at least learn something from this tie-up.

It's likely that the Orange drivers were in the accident lane until they just HAD to move over. Until then, it was the fastest moving lane. Of course, at the last minute they had to change lanes immediately and start inching forward without really waiting for someone to let them into the bumper to bumper traffic. Or perhaps they would be asked to stop and help direct traffic or something important?

It sure made waiting in traffic more fun. But I also had some questions: Would an Orange just make another lane because they were already late? Would they latch onto the next car's bumper to avoid letting anyone in since that would delay them an extra few seconds? Would Golds not let anyone in when they got close, because they should have merged way back? Would a Blue be more likely to let you merge once you've made eye contact and (in a way) connected with them? Wouldn't this have been a great time to survey the Greens thinking through a more efficient way to handle this type of

*congestion? Or did many of them look around, wondering how
stupid many other drivers really were? – J.W.*

Different is neither better or worse, nor right or wrong. For
every instance that our Colors judge someone as being too... there
are many others who think of us as just not being very... The tools
of Colors allow us to look for the good in others and to appreciate
their values and strengths. Without this understanding, our Colors
will continually be labelled. To the world, there are always two
opposing views of how we can see ourselves, and also the ways others
might judge us:

Blues may see themselves as:	*Others may see Blues as:*
Affirming others	A push-over & too nice
Compassionate	Bleeding heart
Creative	Can't see the real world
Empathetic	Easily taken advantage of
Great communicator	Mushy
Idealistic	Naive
Likes to please	Not task oriented & gets sidetracked
People person	Overly emotional
Romantic	Smothering
Social interactions	Soft hearted
Spiritual	Sugar-coats things
Trusting	Talks too much
Wants harmony	Too trusting or soft
Warm & caring	Unrealistic or naïve

Golds may see themselves as:	Others may see Golds as:
Abides by policies	Black or white/ one-tracked
Always has a view	Bossy
Business type	Controlling
Can be counted on	Controls & sets own agenda
Decisive	Dull or boring
Efficient	End justifies the means
Dependable	Judgmental
Goal oriented	Limited flexibility
Great planner	No imagination
Orderly & neat	Opinionated
Practical & stable	Predictable
Provides security	Rigid & often only their way
Realistic	Stubborn
Steady & firm	Stuck in the system
Very organized	Uptight

Oranges may see themselves as:	Others may see Oranges as:
Doesn't get stressed	Always late & off track
Enjoys life	Can't be taken seriously
Flexible	Disobeys rules
Fun loving	Doesn't get focused
Great negotiator	Doesn't know right from wrong
Here and now person	Flaky
Multi-tasking	Irresponsible
New ideas & suggestions	Manipulator
Practical	Problem creator
Problem solver	Shortcuts systems & rule breaker
Resourceful	Tramples over others
Spontaneous	Vague & can't be justified
Winning attitude	Won't follow the plan

Greens may see themselves as:	Others may see Greens as:
Able to reprimand	Aloof & cool
Always right 97% of the time	Arrogant
Calm under pressure	Cold
Creative	Controlled
Efficient	Doesn't care about people
Exact, not repetitive	Finding fault
Firm minded	Hatchet person
Logical decisions	Heartless
Rational	Intellectual snob
Seeking justice	Lacks mercy & caring
Superior intellectually	Not involved in team
Thinking it through	Ruthless
Tough minded	Unfeeling & aloof
Unique & original	Unrealistic

Every day we make decisions about people in less than a minute. We judge them based on our own criteria and values and see them through the filters and glasses of our Colors. If we believe that people come into our lives for a reason, we are ahead of the game already. Is our first reaction that someone is cold and aloof? Or are we prepared to see valuable Greens in much more positive ways than simply being calm and collected?

If we meet an Orange person, full of energy and talking very quickly, what tends to be our first thought? What about the people at work, focused intensely on their current project at hand? Do we think of them as uncaring and totally task-oriented? Or are we prepared to see them as focused, responsible, and invaluable to getting the job done? Do we perceive our Blue friends as always having the time for others and genuinely caring? Or is our initial reaction in the office that there is too much talk and not enough work? Beauty is always in the eye of the beholder.

Persons are Gifts

Persons are gifts of God to me. They are already wrapped. Some beautifully and others less attractively. Some have been mishandled in the mail, others come "special delivery," some are loosely wrapped, and others very tightly enclosed. But the wrapping is not the gift and this is an important realization. It is so easy to make a mistake in this regard, to judge the contents by the cover. Sometimes the gift is opened very easily; sometimes the help of others is needed.

Maybe it is because they are afraid to look inside my wrapping. Maybe I don't trust my own contents. Or it may be that I have never fully accepted the gift that I am. Every meeting and sharing of persons is an exchange of gifts.

My gift is Me; your gift is You. We are gifts to each other.

— Author unknown

Our Shared Strengths and Values

Our different Colors do share a large number of common denominators. For all of us, one combination of Colors or another applies to each of us. For the rest of the world, an understanding of what we share and agree on is always much more valuable than looking for our differences. In all of our relationships, with an open heart and mind, we can easily find common ground with other Colors:

Blue and Orange

These are two people-first Colors who draw their energy from others and believe that paperwork is never as important as their team, friends, coworkers, or clients. Should either of them find themselves in a new city, by the next day they will have met some new friends. Oranges can talk to anyone about anything at a party or networking event, while Blues prefer one-on-one conversations where they can make eye contact and really get to know someone.

As natural optimists, both automatically look at the positive sides of things. They are both very generous and great motivators who avoid negative people and situations whenever possible. They would rather get involved in solving something hands-on than talking about it. Both Colors are also talented negotiators, although in different ways. Oranges succeed in life through their drive to win and by thinking on their feet, while Blues use their gift of intuition and their special talents of building meaningful relationships.

Blues and Oranges share a sense of humor to keep things positive. They both have huge amounts of creativity, and similar beliefs of dreaming the impossible dreams. Both Colors value recognition, and shine brighter when they receive genuine positive feedback for their unique talents and contributions. Oranges enjoy tangible items such as gifts or money while their Blue friends prefer genuine words of affirmation and praise.

Gold and Green

If something needs to be done, it's going to be done right, since these two Colors are process oriented and value logical and efficient ways of doing something – anything. If others have a better idea, they will need to be able to prove it. Both naturally think ahead to any challenges, pitfalls, missing details, or potential problems. If anything does go wrong, both are quite hard on themselves and very self-correcting.

Because Golds and Greens have their credibility on the line, one can bet that any job will be done correctly with a consistent focus on the process and on quality concerns. It is why both Colors can focus intensely on their task at hand, and prefer to work in a quiet area without interruptions. Golds want to get the job done so they can take it off their to-do list while Greens want to do it perfectly the first time, before moving on to something else.

Both Golds and Greens value their privacy and prefer others to get to the point, since neither have much time for small-talk. As task-oriented Colors, in their overall outlook and behavior, both can often put the job to be done ahead of many people issues.

It is also not possible to tell from their faces what is really going on. Both can be accused of not "looking" happy since their demeanor is more business-like or reserved. Greens tend to be calm and cool, while Golds generally have a concerned or focused demeanor.

Green and Orange

On the surface it might not seem that this large group of Orange extroverts and majority of Green introverts have much in common. Yet both are very independent and strong minded and have no problem in challenging authority. Neither of them wants to be told what to do, or how to do something. They will certainly figure it out themselves with their strong self-confidence and "*I can do it*" attitude.

Neither Greens nor Oranges will beat around the bush when they have something to say. They speak their minds in pretty direct ways, without a lot of tolerance for small talk. It is never meant to hurt anyone, and often they cannot understand what might have caused any hurt feelings. Oranges will admit they frequently talk before thinking, and Greens just cannot see how it is logical for someone to get their feelings hurt when they are simply supplying factual information and feedback.

Problem solving is a sport to both of these Colors who enjoy competition and new challenges. They love to compete with anyone – any time, which is greatly motivating and always keeps things interesting and challenging. For Greens it may be the same driving force, but not for the sake of the limelight or attention. It is the mental stimulation of problem-solving and knowing they can do it, but without the fanfare or attention. Their preference is to compete with themselves, or with systems of some kind.

Both Colors love new goals or challenges and avoid mundane and repetitive tasks whenever possible. They do need their space to perform and are eager to seek new ways and methods of doing things: Oranges in seeking to avoid boredom and routines, and Greens to improve and to utilize their ingenuity. It is why Oranges develop many shortcuts to things and Greens invent more efficient ways.

Gold and Blue

These two Colors thrive on their common bond of helping others. They are generous with their time and money for charities and worthy causes, and they make up the vast majority of volunteers. Each gain a large part of their self-esteem by helping their fellow man and lending a hand, which gives them a strong sense of belonging and feeling valued. The motivation of helping take care of others, and doing onto others as they wish to have done for them, makes Golds and Blues great team players. It is something they do without thinking and without selfishness. Both are very protective of their friends and families, and share a strong sense of loyalty.

Golds and Blues both have a hard time saying no to anyone who needs them or who needs help. Yet both also find it very difficult to actually ask for help themselves. *That* somehow seems selfish and they really do not want to impose on others.

For both, conflict of any kind is to be avoided at all costs, since they are rule followers who very much value fitting in without making waves or standing out. What *does* motivate both Golds and Blues is to be appreciated. As very modest Colors, neither wants others to make a big deal about them, but also don't want others to forget them either. When anyone does something nice for them, or offers a genuine thank you, these attitudes of gratitude will certainly be remembered, and go a very long way with these two.

Green and Blue

While Greens function through logic and Blues live in their hearts, these two do share some strong bonds. One of the major common denominators is their great creativity. For Greens it is measured through growth, improving systems or procedures, while Blues focus more on a wide range of artistic areas.

There is a beautiful movie called *Pay It Forward*. It describes a powerful way that Blues make a difference in the lives of others. Greens have that same drive, but do so in a slightly different manner. With their lifelong joy of learning, their way of making a difference is through teaching others. To Greens, a great way of showing someone they care and want to help is by teaching and educating them. While it is a different approach to the same value, it allows both Greens and Blues to leave their mark in the world and to have a positive impact in the lives of others.

Both value a focus on the big picture issues first, before getting into the details and results. They readily see all sides of an issue – since Greens have great lateral thinking skills, and Blues are the consummate and empathetic mediators.

A continuous challenge for these two Colors is to look forward, and not re-live the past. Whether it is re-evaluating decisions from years ago, or lingering hurt feelings, Blues and Greens need to stay mindful that they cannot live for a better past. It is an issue compounded for anyone with Blue and Green as their highest Color combination.

Gold and Orange

Golds and Oranges would rather act than talk. They share a strong sense of impatience and a need to get on with something: *"Tell me what to do and let me do it."* Both function for today and want to focus on the job at hand without "wasting" too much time and energy on long range ideas or visions. Their strong bonds are their abilities to work well in teams. Golds contribute by helping and serving others out of a sense of duty and by getting the job done. Oranges make things happen with their people-oriented nature, enthusiasm, and flexibility. Now if others could just share their drive to work hard…

On the surface it might seem these two have a very different definition of friendship. Oranges do have a lot of friends and they certainly know a ton of people through their networking groups. But like their Gold buddies, whose definition of friends is two or three lifelong friends, *that* is the same number who actually know the real Orange person in any meaningful way. Golds may be very private people in the first place, but for Oranges who seem to know everyone, few people actually know them well.

Together, these two really value being in charge and in control: Oranges with their strong personalities and Golds with their steadfast definition of right and wrong. Both measure a large part of their successes through money, even though they totally disagree on what to do with it after they have earned it.

The Journey for Balance

The power of understanding the tools and insights of Colors starts within each of us. Perhaps it is putting words and definitions with many things we always knew, but never had the words to express or describe. The next, and more important step, is to have an open heart and mind to look for the value and the good in others. It comes about through choosing to see other Colors as a gift and a blessing.

All of us naturally see the world through the eyes of our Colors. For the majority of people, living life in balance requires patience, practice, and a willingness to look at others a little differently. It comes through a desire to do more of what works, and less of what doesn't in our lives:

- Understand our strengths and know which of these we can take to extremes where they can potentially become a problem, instead of a blessing.

- Always remember the unique values and joys within other's Colors. Take the time to communicate and appreciate them on their terms and in ways others value and understand.

- Stay mindful that most people do not share our personality type. At times, their words, actions, and behaviors are not ones we share. We always need to stay aware of our judgements or reactions to such situations.

We cannot control or change others, or their actions or reactions. We can, however, teach them about Colors, and the preferences and challenges inherent within each Color. Nobody chooses to annoy us on purpose. When others understand us a little better, they will be much more likely to stay out of their judgments. As a result, our Color conflicts will be greatly minimized, and our relationships will improve.

Could you, or are you willing to, flex or stretch today? Can you do something today which is a little out of the comfort zone of your Colors? The challenge would be to do one thing a little differently. It needs to be small enough that you actually do it, but large enough that you will notice.

Nothing about Colors will or should change anyone. Each of us is unique and special as a first-rate version of who we are. We should never attempt to become a second-rate version of someone else. But there is a time and a place for everything and every Color. Life in balance creates a journey of growth and self-improvement when:

Your Blue consistently shows in you caring for others, and reaching out to them. You involve everyone around you and give from the heart – to your friends, family, and others. Your kindness and communication skills touch everyone you come into contact with. Your genuine warmth, empathy, and teamwork skills are contagious and impact those around you. You make lasting friendships and are always ready, willing, and able to make time for others.

Your Gold stands out in your loyalty, dependability, and special talents to take on tasks and see them through to completion. Your strong sense of right and wrong, work ethic, and planning, are qualities others appreciate. Your word is always good and you function well with deadlines without supervision. You work at the same time as both an individual and as a team player, and people can always count on you to help wherever and whenever you're needed.

Your Orange is the energy and positive outlook that everyone admires. You have a contagious sense of humor and teach others that anything is possible through your practical actions, and high energy level. Your ability to multi-task and your gift of flexibility, without stress, is valued and envied by those that watch you in action. You are never afraid to roll up your sleeves and get involved in practical and creative ways that only you can pull off.

Your Green pursues challenges and solutions, constantly seeking improvements and keeping your eye on the big picture and broader visions. Your range of knowledge goes far beyond your job, and it is well known and respected. You continue to learn and to grow, always seeking opportunities to share your broad knowledge and well thought out ideas and suggestions with others.

Or to summarize:

> Embrace yourself as you are…
> Just for today –
> make your Gold lists shorter,
> nurture your Blue relationships,
> value and grow your Green knowledge
> and treasure your Orange freedom.

Sure, we have lots in common — like that we're both impatient.
I want to get it done and off my list and you want
to get it done because you're bored.

I know you're concerned and nervous, but when I said we should
talk, I just meant about my dreams and feelings and stuff.

Chapter Eight

Relationships: Love is Colorblind

"We can order both and then we can split it."
"What if I just want what I want?"
"Honey, you gave that up when we married."
Kelsey Restaurant Ad

In relationships, opposites attract. Way more than half of all couples are in a relationship with a spouse of a totally different Color. Consciously, or often unconsciously, we look for someone who has the skills or strengths that we may not have. More often than not, we are attracted to someone whose personality traits complement ours, which creates that strong sense: *we can do anything – if we just do it together.*

A loving and healthy relationship is like a little piece of heaven right here on earth. Yet, healthy relationships do not happen by accident. They require commitment, effective communication, hard work, and many other tools and building blocks in order for two people to grow together as a couple. While Colors is not a dating tool, it does create a deeper understanding of our partner's strengths, stresses, and values. What we see with our spouses, really is what we get. But what do we want from our relationships? What traits do we most admire in our partners, and alternatively, what issues create stress in their actions, inactions, or behaviors? Knowing is always better than hoping because our partners are not going to come around, change their Colors, or somehow transform themselves to become more like us.

Is the wish of somehow changing our partner a possible part of the reason why our divorce rate is over 40 percent? Is there a point in year one, five, or ten when one partner starts to spend more and more of their energy attempting to make the other person more like them? If so, it becomes a slippery slope of trouble when our initial attractions turn to focusing our energies and efforts into "fixing" our partner's traits or behaviors.

For second marriages, the divorce rate rises to more than 60 percent. So the second time around, we make a worse relationship decision? As if any divorce is not painful enough! Yet opposites still attract, but more often than not, we still do not have a clear understanding of what that really encompasses. We never did get an owners-manual for our partner, or even the words to define many of our own behaviors and stresses.

Who does each Color tend to marry? While the chart below is not definitive, the survey results are from sufficiently large numbers of seminar attendees and have significant validity.

Partner's Primary Color

Primary Color

	Green	Gold	Orange	Blue
Gold	22%	27%	24%	27%
Orange	43%	12%	24%	21%
Blue	24%	30%	14%	32%
Green	29%	27%	38%	6%

*Who do we date or marry? Challenges can arise in
any relationship, regardless of our partner's Colors.
Will we remember the beautiful traits that we were
first attracted to? Will we still value them years
from now? If so, love is always colorblind.*

Honest, open, and effective communication always is, and will be, one of the main building blocks of successful relationships. Along with every Color's desire for quality time together, communication is the most frequently cited factor in the strengthening or the weakening of relationships.

If communication is one of the key factors for growth, it can also be a prime area of conflict when we tend to think, "*I communicate really well, it's just that my partner doesn't.*" How often do we want to be right, instead of happy, or choose to talk solely in the ways of our own Colors, instead of communicating in the ways our partner actually values and understands? Can doing the same thing over and over ever reach a different result?

Many times, seemingly simple communications with our partner of a different Color can quickly go off the rails. It may not seem like a big deal at the time, but like unraveling a sweater, hurt feelings linger, our partner withdraws, and the battle lines are drawn. Oranges may raise their voices in frustration, or make fun of something or someone. For Oranges, this is never a big deal and is quickly forgotten. However, with a Gold or Green partner, criticism in public (at work, with friends, or in front of their family) is often perceived as a personal attack.

Blues, the vast majority of whom are women, can feel frustrated, unheard, or unloved when their husbands (mostly Greens and Golds) are not very good mind readers. These Gold and Green men are really adept at fixing and solving things. However, neither Color is likely to ever fully bridge the gap between the feelings-related, "*if you loved me you would know...*" and the logical, "*what exactly do you want me to do?*" (For more insights, *The Colors of Relationship* booklet includes worksheets on each Color's common stresses with their partner to create a meaningful dialogue for all relationship combinations.)

As the stats of relationship combinations show, love truly is colorblind. While that is the great news, and always does hold true, a divorce rate of more than 40 percent makes it clear that our Colors can also be deaf and blind – deaf, in not learning to speak the "language" of our partners, and blind in not seeing their Colors.

Do You Have the Time?

Each and every day we take the time to get ourselves ready in the morning. We take the time to shower, get dressed to look good, and take care of ourselves. Every day we make the time to go to work, to go out with our friends, and to watch our favorite television shows. Even if our television died today, we would make it a priority to buy a new one before tomorrow.

We choose to make the time to learn a new sport or hobby. We take two, three, or four years to earn our degree. We invest years of work to earn a promotion, almost two decades to raise our kids, and even longer to save for our retirement.

But somehow we often take our relationship for granted and expect it to grow stronger without the same efforts. Invest the time – use the tools of Colors – and spend the same amount of energy in your relationship as in other areas of your life. It is worth it, your partner is worth it, and it will be one of the best investments you can make.

The Rainbow of Relationship Combinations

What exactly is the best combination of Colors in a relationship? The answer is simple: it is exactly the unique combination each couple has. Every relationship combination includes a long list of gifts and strengths, as well as challenges with differing viewpoints, or preferences. A common understanding of Colors contributes in a multitude of ways to any couple's life-long growth towards becoming a loving and unstoppable team. All that is needed is an open heart and mind, along with the willingness to learn and grow together.

When two people enter into a relationship, it always combines two distinct personalities. Some merge easily, while others require more flexibility, but every combination benefits greatly with an "owners-manual" to each other's Colors. Even in marriage counseling, the evolving approach is less about focusing on changes, and more on creating an understanding between spouses. A powerful tool for that foundation begins with understanding each other:

Blue and Gold: Doing it right or feeling good about it?

Blues and Golds make up vast numbers of couples. When this relationship works well, it is a beautiful balance between getting the job done and caring about others. After all, these two are the largest groups of volunteers who believe in helping their fellow man and taking care of others in their community by sharing their gifts of time, talents, and money.

This couple places a great priority on their family and friends, and shares a huge sense of loyalty towards them. Golds have a much smaller group of three or four life-long friends, whereas their Blue partners seem to collect them. Golds are just more reserved, and are often amazed at how easily their partners can make friends in such genuine ways.

The Blue gift of giving, caring, and sharing unconditionally is something their Gold partner will quickly learn. After all, Blues love them for who they are, not for what they do, their high expectations, or their lofty standards. Blues will soften the Gold's drive to work harder and to do more. They know that happiness is always a journey and not a Gold destination.

At first, this may be a challenge for Golds to accept since, in their view, hard work and a completed to-do list equals success. They worry a lot and work to ensure everything gets done, that they are saving enough, and even whether or not they are being a good enough parent. They even worry about what to plan for this coming weekend. How can their partners say not to worry, or that all the stuff which still has to get done is not a big deal? It might be great to hear, but Golds will need to hear it often before learning to soften their thinking. Is it possible that even love is something Golds need to earn, in the same way that fun is earned at the end of their list of chores? To every Blue, love is unconditional, and it is never based on accomplishments.

What a powerful influence for Golds to know that their Blue partners will always put people and feelings ahead of any paperwork or task, even at the expense of their own needs and feelings. But then, this is an area where Golds can be a great help and sometimes be the "bad guy," to set boundaries, say no, and make sure their Blue partners *do* take care of themselves first.

Setting boundaries, or just being direct and to the point, is easy for Golds, who will say, "*tomorrow we need to…*" It is harder for Blues who word their questions or requests in a much softer manner, such as, "*we should maybe….*" Golds are action-oriented, and a "*we should*" likely has Golds out of their seat and immediately starting to move. With an understanding of each other's communication methods there is always value in compromising between a direct, order-like approach, and the soft may-never-be-heard method. Until then, Blues will sometimes get to the point of frustration or crying before they will feel heard or understood.

The Blue partner is definitely more of a big-picture dreamer, and much more creative. Their relationship will grow in measurable ways when Golds use their practicality skills and process-oriented views to encourage their partner's big dreams. They must looks for ways to support Blues, and not cut down their dreams to realistic terms. In return, Blues will be able to supply the people-first view and creative options to the frequent Gold black or white mindset and decision-making style.

Green and Blue: Think it through or feel it?

With these two Colors, the vast range of living in the heart and living through logic is well covered, and both value the stability of their committed relationship. The Blue partner is certainly the care-giver, as well as the caretaker, and the heart of the relationship. He or she will remember birthdays, anniversaries, and social occasions. The Blue partner will probably also build a very close relationship with his or her in-laws, who are not accustomed to many of the special people touches from their Green son or daughter.

Blues will probably take on the majority of housework, shopping, and things around the house that make it feel more like a home. Many of these are the little things Greens certainly enjoy, even though it may be hard to understand their importance at times. Blues take many things off their Green partner's plate that seem to be tiny but important in the relationship. Until then, a Green single person will often eat irregularly and may go a long time without buying new clothes, or even giving much thought to housework.

All those great Blue gifts allow their Green partners to stay focused on the big issues of life and not have to deal with the perceived tedious or mundane daily needs and tasks. When it comes to things like dinner parties, or lots of time with friends and family, it will likely be the Blues who make the social events happen.

The Green need for some alone-time every day is difficult for Blues to understand. It takes a long time to stop feeling as though they have done something wrong. Blues, however, are very proud of the intelligence and calm demeanor of their partners. He or she is a true friend they can lean on, and that will help to set boundaries to keep them from over committing. Their partners can also be a great help in finding simple and logical solutions, and can bring blown-out-of-proportion problems back down to their real size.

Greens are people of few words who prefer to deal with logic and facts. Do not expect them to talk from their heart without filtering the words. That is a gift exclusive to Blues. Greens will always talk about facts and logic, which can result in some rather direct feedback and hurt feelings. Yet, these comments are made because Greens love their Blue partners, because they want them to do better, think better, and have better information. They are never intended to be hurtful. Since Greens love to learn, these areas of their relationships will grow much stronger if and when they adapt some of the softer Blue communication tools.

With Blues there will certainly be a roller coaster of emotions long past the logical Green expiry date. Greens love to study people and are pattern-seekers who often understand their Blue partners better than their partners seems to know themselves. But it will continue to be a puzzle how quickly feelings can get hurt, why simple things get taken to heart, and why going along just to get along can be such a priority to a Blue.

Finally, as important as an hour of alone time is for Greens, four hugs a day are even more critical to Blues. Physical touch, cuddling on the sofa, holding hands, and their four hugs a day are not optional. They are as critical as oxygen is to breathing. Yes, Blues will sometimes nag to get a Green to see this critical relationship builder, but at that point they can also refuse the physical closeness. It may not seem logical, but Greens have to want to want it, and not do so out of a sense of obligation. When this is an integral part of their daily life, Blues will feel loved beyond anything words or logic can express.

Orange and Gold: Should we wing it or make a plan?

If opposites attract, this couple is certainly a prime example. It is the powerful combination of an Orange multi-tasker who is a flexible and eternally optimistic, together with a Gold who will take care of the planning and structure, and takes both very seriously. Oranges contribute endlessly through their ideas and creativity, along with their positive energy and networking skills. Their Gold partners are much happier away from the limelight, staying behind the scenes, and taking care of the details in the relationship.

With so much on the go, Oranges are very grateful to have Golds who care, because someone needs to do that stuff – it just won't be them. As long as paperwork and structure does not become a priority, take away their need for freedom, or impose a lot of "have to" rules, Oranges will gladly let their partners handle the details.

Golds value their Orange partner's hands-on skills, flexibility, and ability to work well under stress. They marvel at Orange's *No Fear and Just Do It* attitudes, consistently positive outlook, and never accepting *no* for an answer. Golds watch Oranges try almost anything without a firm plan – even talking to total strangers in any situation

– and are often left shaking their heads in amazement. It can actually be a little embarrassing for Golds, but it is one of the many reasons they are so proud of their Orange partner's talents.

As with everything in life, there is a time and a place for everything and the issues of flexibility versus planning can often arise. Golds may have their whole Saturday planned out, but if something better comes along, would they be willing to stay flexible and change plans? After dinner, when their Orange partners might be getting restless and want to get out of the house *"right now,"* could those impulsive decisions come with a thirty-minute timer? Can Golds get the time to load the dishwasher, clean up the kitchen, and complete their to-do list? Perhaps a challenge for Golds would be to not appear to make the relationship more important than the dishes.

When both partners find the compromise between living for the moment and planning the next moment, their relationship will continue to grow. After all, some holiday planning, for example, is valuable. But any Orange will have way more fun getting there, or getting lost, and exploring a ton of places they would never have seen if they had followed a fixed agenda. What a joy it is to learn together, that *"don't worry be happy"* really is valuable, even though staying on track and having a plan before jumping into action can sometimes avoid headaches and mistakes. Many times, one person will see opportunities, while the other sees the pitfalls. When both get on the same wavelength, these two become a much stronger team.

This couple certainly enjoys making a lot of money. Where they differ is whether this money should be saved and invested, or spent on buying toys. Through trial and error (and maybe a few fights), both will find a workable compromise. This will lie somewhere between the Orange impulse-shopping style of *see it – want it – buy it*, and the Gold sensibility of wanting a good deal, comparison shopping, or squirreling away a lot of savings for that guaranteed rainy day. Golds are quite conservative with money while Oranges know there will always be more where that came from.

Green and Orange: Just do it or think about it?

For this team, controlling the other person is never going to happen. Both are very independent in their own unique ways, something they discovered about each other on their first date. Greens never want to be told what to think and Oranges have no hesitation shutting down anyone who attempts to tell them what to do.

For Greens, Oranges are almost a mystery to be studied or solved. Their partners are the outgoing, active, and impulsive people in the relationship who shoot from the hip, network with anyone and everyone, and thrive on a life of social interactions. Greens are always amazed, since few of those traits apply to them. Parties are rare and impulse actions, or talking without thinking it through first, do not happen. Outgoing? – Well, not so much. Even at a party, both will enjoy the night in very different ways. Oranges are looking to meet a dozen people that they can hit up for a fundraiser, or who might become future clients. Their Green partners would much rather wander off in search of that one person who can discuss the validity of Neuro Linguistic programming for a couple of hours, away from the party.

Oranges quickly recognize that large parts of their social lives may happen without their spouse, who would rather stay at home with a good book or work on the computer. For Greens, to have some alone time is a treat, while Oranges think of it as more of a punishment. The drive to *"let's go do something"* will usually start with the Orange partner, although what they actually do may include some things a Green has always wanted to see or explore.

Oranges will often talk first and think later when they shoot from the hip and think through their ideas while talking. When these creative and off-the-cuff ideas are filtered through the mind of their Green partners, they will be amended, fixed, fleshed out, and perfected. How great it is to have the creative ideas of an Orange run through the computer analysis of a Green mind.

When working together this way, both will learn a lot from each other. However, Oranges need to remember that their partners are not killing their ideas or vision. When Greens are correcting their spelling, grammar, or ideas, it is not from a mindset of criticism or control. It is done out of love, because their Green partners want them to have better information, sound more credible, or to make better decisions.

A final area of conflict often revolves around what to wear or how to shop. Oranges love the latest, coolest fashions while Greens tend to place little value on things so trivial. Just wearing anything is often good enough and not worth a lot of time or thought. On the other hand, something more important, such as a new car or laptop, does take some time – not the two-hour Orange way of shopping, but rather spending the time to research even before heading to a store. Anyone wagering on shopping decisions between these two should bet more on the Green person speeding up, than any Orange slowing down.

Gold and Green: Take it off the list or make it perfect?

This couple is definitely focused on task-oriented issues with concrete actions, tangible results, quality work, and a great sense of accomplishment. People and their feelings may take a back seat to practicality and getting the job done, and done right.

Golds benefit greatly from their partner's love of learning, finding more efficient solutions, and seeing options in more than black or white terms. They are also able to emulate the typical Green calm demeanor by avoiding stress over small issues, and focusing on the big picture as much as their to-do lists.

In return, Greens will have someone who can ground them and keep them on track by viewing life in realistic terms and practical solutions. If Greens had the choice, thinking something through could go on for an extended period while their Gold partners keep pushing for closure. Greens will be more relaxed, and often passive in the relationship, while Golds are the on-the-go people with definite ideas of what has to be done and when.

Where this couple can see things quite differently is whether something should get done now, or done perfectly. Whether it is fixing the garage door or any other renovation project, this question can become a problem. To Golds, once something is decided, started, and on their to-do list, it needs to be finished – now! That can make for long days, or even hiring someone, but the prime motivation is to get the job completed. This is not their partner's mindset or goal. Tinkering, experimenting, taking some time to research options, or getting some feedback at the home improvement store, can make this a fun and rewarding project. But it will always get done right, and not be based on an artificial timetable pushing for closure.

It will also be Golds who take care of the practical and daily tasks, such as shopping, cleaning, and family dinners. Thanks to Golds, parties and family celebrations are planned well in advance with no details left to chance. Gifts are bought, wrapped, and sent on time – every time. This is all the stuff that Greens know should be important, but may not be their priority.

The definition of organization consists of neat piles and labeled boxes to Golds, but more mental organization for Greens. For that reason, it helps when Greens have their own space somewhere in the house. The expression *"everything in its place"* is not one Greens share or want to adapt, which can drive their Gold partners nuts. Greens do need a place to have their alone-time, get on the computer, read, or just relax. Alone-time is an integral part of their personal to-do list, yet Golds can act as though this Green time should somehow be earned after their *real* to-do list is finished.

Orange and Blue: Get over it or let the feelings linger?

These two people-first Colors care first and foremost about all of their relationships and friendships. Blues build their self-esteem through the depth of their emotions, intimacy, and meaningful relationships and always make the time for others. Their Orange partners just get there more quickly and prefer large numbers of friends, without getting too bogged down in the depth of other relationships, or having to answer a bunch of open-ended feelings-type questions.

Both partners have deep-seated feelings and passions. Blues are frequently drawn to the Orange sense of humor, and the ability to quickly (and painlessly) leave the past in the past. At some point this can cause conflict when Blues feel their Orange partners may not take their feelings seriously enough, or understand their need to re-live events, conversations, or hurt feelings. It's true; Oranges do not always understand why Blues cannot just get over it and get on with life. *Please – life's too short.* Yet, Blues can sometimes misinterpret this mindset as uncaring.

Oranges want to be taken at face value and, accordingly, treat others in the same manner. They seldom linger about hidden meanings or listen for what is not being said. If they do not understand something, or want to know anything, they will ask a direct question. This can make their Blue partners shudder. *Cut to the chase and get to the point?* This is a hard thing for Blues to do, even though they are often a little envious. In real life, it would just be rude and impolite. Blues analyze conversations, deeper meanings, or the real feelings behind the words, but do appreciate that the Orange's directness leaves much less room for misunderstandings. The great trade-off is that Blues can learn to become more direct, while being the translators for their Orange partners. Blues can be the early-warning system when feelings are hurt, or when patience and sensitivity is needed.

In any of their relationships, Oranges are very direct about most issues. Blues now have someone who can set boundaries for them and say *no* where they just can't. The Blue intuition knows that their partners love them and care for them deeply, even if they have a really hard time standing still and just talking things through – without multi-tasking, getting sidetracked, cracking a joke, or bottom-lining the conversation. The challenge for Blues is not to make their Orange partners feel trapped or confined. When Oranges sense this boxed-in feeling, it is possible for them to run or quit on the relationship.

Blues look for quality time together by just cuddling on the sofa or holding hands. Since these require Oranges to stop multi-tasking, Blues need to create these specific times in healthy, win-win ways. If Blues appear needy or clingy, Oranges may start tuning out in order to protect their need for freedom, which compounds matters when their partners really get their feelings hurt. Blues have deep running feelings and emotions; they look for the good in everyone and will forgive and forgive. They will not easily forget, however. Getting their feelings hurt too often can result in them building up walls in order to protect themselves.

In their careers, both Colors likely have people-first jobs and can become hugely successful in using their natural skills of building relationships. Since neither enjoys the mundane jobs in life, things do get a lot easier at home when this couple hires someone to do their housework, taxes, and investments. Someone has to – it just should not be either of these two partners.

Gold and Gold: *Taking care of business*

These two Golds likely started their relationship through a friendship, and probably dated for an extended period of time. Neither partner would quickly jump into a relationship without an extended test-drive while getting to know the other, often over a number of years. Once in a relationship, this is definitely the "getting it done" team. Together, these two will accomplish anything they set their minds to, with focus and unwavering determination. Both are primarily task-oriented and prefer to plan, execute, and move on. There is not any discussion or wasted time when they are on task and on the job.

This couple finds comfort and security in the tried and true established routines of their lives. It may not seem like fun to others, but for these two, it is. After all, fun, or quality of life, is always in the eye of the beholder. A neat and organized home, the yard work done, and all the bills paid are the steps to having fun and relaxing. Until then, there is work to be done before they can relax and enjoy themselves.

Both partners have strong leadership skills and prefer to be the decision-makers in the relationship. Neither likes to be told what to do, or presented with a ready-made decision. Their disagreements are not about what needs to get done, but more about how to do it, and the order of different priorities. Most times, Gold couples prefer a clear and specific division of duties around the house which also helps to avoid many conflicts. Of course they will help each other; Golds love acts of service and will gladly pitch in, instead of talking about it. But at the end of the day, someone does need to be accountable, responsible, and in charge.

Learning to share the duties and responsibilities, as well as being open to the wishes of their partners, are valuable lessons for this Gold team. In fact, one partner may sometimes start to exhibit a few traits which seem to go against his or her first Color. This may be a default into their second Color, or another way to feel in control. It can range from adapting a habit of being late to not finishing tasks or projects.

It is likely both partners are involved with service clubs, their church, community groups, or other charities. Golds are the largest group of volunteers who feel a strong obligation to give back to society. Their shared sense of duty and responsibility may be the reason they first volunteered. But, it will quickly become a sense of purpose and belonging when Golds contribute their time and talents in their communities.

Golds are very good with money and saving. They share conservative and traditional values and feel safe and loved knowing that they can trust each other unconditionally to always be good to their word and honor their promises. Golds strongly believe in traditions and the institution of marriage – for better or worse and definitely until death do us part – no matter what.

Orange and Orange: The power couple makes it happen

Action and adventure are two appropriate adjectives to describe this power couple. Unlike their Gold friend's traditional dating time, these two probably sped up the process, a lot. Their abilities to make quick decisions often extends to the way they enter into their relationships – the Orange energy, networking, and need to always be on the go – times two! This is certainly one of the most high-energy couples that others will be hard-pressed to keep up with.

Both partners are game to try almost anything and everything and live life by their own rules. With every relationship, our second Color matters a lot, which is especially true with these two. An Orange/Gold partner will want to play, but will also be in charge of making up the rules. A Blue second Color will be more sensitive to hurt feelings and act cautiously when talking first and dealing with the potential fallout later. And an Orange/Green partner can quickly flip from impulse decisions to perfectionism, looking to have a certain amount of alone time, or becoming more self-critical.

If competition is healthy and leads to more success and rewards, an Orange now has a partner that will put up a good fight and become a great motivator. Sports, conversations, and work can now be turned into a competition and a game to win. Together, both will feed off each other's competitive drive and winning attitude. *"What can go wrong?"* or *"we can do anything,"* will often be their mindset.

With their desire for freedom, at least one partner will likely be self-employed, or certainly in some type of sales or commission-based career. Using their networking skills and vast circle of friends, business will be good and both will be successful. This team is definitely about working hard and playing hard, with the freedom to come and go as they please. Part of this drive is also necessary in order to make a ton of money, because both Oranges know how to spend. They are very generous, but money comes and goes quickly. Money is really not meant for savings, but to buy toys, cars, or clothes, and certainly to eat out a lot.

In an argument or fight with these two Oranges, we could likely sell tickets. Both will tell it like it is without holding back. But we'd have to get there in a hurry because arguments might blow up suddenly, and can be resolved just as quickly. There will not be any pent-up anger or lingering hurt feelings, and the next day neither partner may even remember what caused the fight. They tend to get it out, get it on, and get it over with just as quickly.

A great stress-avoider for Orange couples is to hire others to take care of the routine and mundane things in their lives. Within their own offices, there is likely someone Gold with strong organizational skills to manage all the details, which just give Oranges a headache. At home, simply having a cleaning person is a huge treat since both would like a clean and neat house, but would prefer not to be the ones doing it.

Green and Green: *The thinking couple*

A relationship of two Greens is rare, indeed. Green females are a tiny percentage of the population, which makes it difficult for these two to find each other (often in or around college or university campuses). When they do meet, both are happy to finally be with someone who truly understands them. These two will have a relaxed and easygoing style since neither partner will be too hung up on mundane matters. What or when to eat, what to wear, or being stuck with too many chores, are just not much of a priority.

Both Greens love their independence and value being with someone who shares their need for space without pushing or nagging them. Their home will have a fair amount of hi-tech gadgets and probably the latest and greatest computers. What better way to spend their alone-time than getting on the computer or reading? Others may not understand, but this couple is not above e-mailing or text messaging each other, even when both are at home.

With their Green thirst for knowledge and lifelong drive to grow, these two love discussions and stimulating conversations. Both will continuously motivate each other's drive for knowledge and understanding, and will certainly learn a lot from each other. In their smaller circle of friends or coworkers, this includes spirited exchanges with others who can match their intellect, who might be experts in their fields, or knowledgeable about something of interest to Greens.

To other Colors or their families, it can seem that the warmth or physical touch exhibited by other couples seems to be missing. True. These two Greens are not likely to hold hands, kiss in public, or show much emotion. While every Green feels and cares just as deeply as anyone else, their external public demeanor will be more reserved. However, that can never be used as a measuring tool for the depth of their relationship.

Blue and Blue: The feeling and caring couple

Similar to Green couples, this is another example of an infrequent relationship, since Blue males are as rare as Green females. The depth and total commitment to each other shows very clearly in this Blue-Blue team. A double Blue relationship involves a total focus on taking care of each other and their many shared values. This special team tends to survive the test of time since both partners are intuitively attuned to each other's needs, dreams, and emotions. Building a strong and lasting relationship just comes naturally for these two who share an unwavering desire to make a difference in the lives of others.

For this Blue couple, life is all about each other and their shared feelings. Few things are nicer than being able to escape the sometimes cruel world and go home to someone who truly understands their roller coaster of emotions and strong intuition. What is hard, however, is being able to say *no* and to set boundaries. But at least they have someone who truly understands these challenges. It does take a lot for Blues to exhibit any selfishness or acting-out behaviors. During those times, it is important that their Blue partners are not also pulled down emotionally.

Neither partner requires or values control, or finds any need for power struggles. To Blues, relationships are all about sharing, caring, being good listeners, and laughing and crying together. Both have each other as their first priority and know they will always have a safe haven from the world when they are together. Or in the words of the old Captain and Tennille song: *"Love will keep us together."*

Relationship Hurdles

Along with the vast array of beautiful gifts each Color contributes to a relationship, there are also some common challenges. None of these arise from a mindset of wanting to make trouble; they are simply natural parts of our Colors. But as any Green will tell you, knowledge is power and we can never change or heal what we do not understand or acknowledge:

Blue Challenges

When Blues fall in love, they fall head over heals in love – unconditionally, all consuming, and often with no boundaries or limits. It makes their partners very blessed to have such unqualified support and encouragement. The downside for Blues is that they can put their relationships above their own needs.

- *Look after yourself first. Selfish as that may sound, that is not the case at all. You give, and keep giving to everyone around you, yet have nothing left for yourself. As a result, you can get that run-down feeling. In small and gentle ways, can you learn to set boundaries and to say no at times? You will always be much healthier, and better able to reach out to others, when you first take care of yourself. It really will create an awesome sense of freedom; and only when you take better care of yourself can you take better care of others.*

- *Understand when an issue is not about you or about feelings. Yes, that is certainly easier said than done since turning off your emotions is never possible. After all, you cannot tell your heart what to think. But if your partner says or does certain things, is your first reaction to make it about hurt feelings which can cloud your judgments? How often could it be about facts, instead of feelings?*

- *Your best is all you have. What really hurts are those frequent feelings that you have not done enough, or somehow you could have done more. In each situation, and with each person, you can only give 100 percent. When you truly believe that, it will show in your demeanor, self-confidence, and the way you feel about yourself. Trust and believe that when you do your best, God does the rest.*

For other Colors blessed enough to be with a Blue partner, there is one additional challenge to remember: the silent treatment after a disagreement or argument is one of the biggest Blue relationship killers. Walking out or going away may seem like a good idea at the time, but will have the opposite effect. The silent treatment makes things worse, much worse for the person we care about the most in life.

We can always take half an hour to cool down, get frustrated, stomp our feet, even yell, or walk around the block. But then, we need to focus on healing and resolving the conflict. Take our Blue partner's hands, sit across from him or her, make eye contact, and talk openly and honestly. Do not let go of their hands until the issue has been resolved. For Blues, absence does not make the heart grow fonder, it makes things worse. Time does not heal all wounds, it only builds scar tissue. And simply forgetting the issue will not bring Blues forgiveness, healing, or resolution.

Gold Challenges

Golds take all relationships very seriously and are loyal friends and spouses. While dating, they are fully committed and can seem to be off their agenda, but this flexibility may be limited. At some point, Golds tend to get back to their focus of the tasks at hand, which their partners can falsely interpret as taking their relationships for granted.

- *Put aside your agenda more often. Sometimes, many times, it is better to just go with the flow. You typically believe that most changes in plans or agreements should not happen. When your partner has a change of heart, or wants to make different plans, honor him or her by going along with his or her wishes and by staying flexible. Who knows? It might be fun or interesting if you remain willing and open-minded, and it will certainly strengthen your relationship.*

- *Understand that not everyone shares your strong drive to be on time, every time. When people rely on you, being on time is simply common courtesy. Does that need to include being on time for a movie, party, or concert? What's the worst that can happen if you are not? You would miss the preview ads or ten minutes of a warm-up band. Making a big deal out of a little deal by pressuring your partner to stay on time creates stress and tension. Communicate honestly and openly the specific times where on-time really does matter. Then be willing to compromise when late is not really late, or can be perceived as being more important than your relationship.*

- *Recognize that others see the world in various shades of gray. To you, much of life can be black or white, right or wrong. For better or worse, it is not a perspective which other Colors share. Be ready and willing to look at more issues in your relationship through the eyes of your partner. After all, wouldn't you rather be happy than right?*

Orange Challenges

Oranges add variety and excitement to any relationships. They are generous, action-oriented, and eternal optimists. In their drive for freedom, Oranges may have a tendency to give up on a relationship when they start feeling tied down or being controlled.

- *Not everything is fun. It can be a challenge when your partner cannot readily tell when you have turned serious. The rest of the world cannot change tracks as easily as you can. Your friends, coworkers, and partner can find it hard to keep up, or to realize when you have switched gears.*

- *Fight fair. You have a strong drive to win and to be a winner. Disagreements with your partner should not be the time to make winning your primary goal. You can make fights really nasty or tune out with your favorite last word: "whatever!" It might just drag out the fight or escalate it for no reason. Is it really important that they lose and that you win? Will the end result not just be lose-lose anyway?*

- *Hang in there longer. Let's be honest, you like things fast and immediate. In your relationship this can sometimes become an issue. When things are not going well, you have a tendency to quit. You can also get that nagging feeling that maybe there is something more out there beyond being tied-down or committed. Sometimes it is important to fully think things through, or count to 100, before voting with your feet.*

Green Challenges

Greens initial interests in relationships may not always start on a romantic or emotional level. They value knowledge and intelligence and can first be attracted to someone who is able to mentally challenge them. This person should also have a match to their intelligence level, without the need for a lot of external validation.

- *Speak from the heart. Yes, you find it difficult to talk about emotions, but you do know that it is of great importance to the large group of the world who communicates from their heart. Share your feelings and allow your partner to see your heart and your feelings. It contributes greatly to closer bonds and a stronger relationship, even thought it may not seem logical. Besides, what's the worst that could happen when you trust your partner with your feelings?*

- *Calm, cool, and collected is difficult for others to understand or to appreciate. They do value your calm demeanor, but many times, your partner and others would rather experience your caring and gentle side. It does strengthen relationships when you trust some people enough to let them see that often hidden side of you.*

- *Teach others the meaning of Green alone-time. It is not optional, and one way or another you assure that you do get it. Rather than simply fading away, teach your partner what your needs are. This is your time to unwind and process your day. Your partner or others can wonder if you are mad or uninterested. It will be up to you to educate them about the value of alone-time, because they may not understand, or share its importance.*

Fast Does Not Always Work

Since acting and entertaining are prime careers for many Oranges, no insights into relationships would be complete without a look at Hollywood.

One of Canada's better known exports to the U.S., Pamela Anderson, married rocker Tommy Lee after having known him for four days, filing for divorce within a year. In October 2007, Anderson married Rick Salomon during the hour plus break between her Vegas shows. It was already the third marriage for both. After two months, Anderson filed for divorce but three days later had the papers withdrawn since they were attempting to reconcile. Yet within five months, all bets were off and the annulment was complete.

Michelle Phillips, ex-singer of the Mamas & Papas lasted eight days with actor Dennis Hopper. In her words, *"It was the happiest eight days of my life."* Nicolas Cage and Lisa Marie Presley easily surpassed that time, staying together for three months.

Drew Barrymore's first five-week marriage was to bar owner Jeremy Thomas whom she had met six weeks earlier and decided to marry within a few hours. It was followed by her marriage to actor Tom Green twice (don't ask...) which lasted a year. That was followed by a "long-term" relationship to drummer Fabrizio Moretti, but these days, insiders quote Barrymore as saying that she is not interested in another serious relationship.

Britney Spears is one of the highest selling female singers in the world, yet her self-destructive behaviors have also been well documented. Her very public four year relationship with Justin Timberlake was followed by a 5 A.M. marriage to childhood friend Jason Alexander which lasted two days. Nine months later, Spears married Kevin Federline, and that breakup was certainly well covered by the media.

> *"Six months to heal from a breakup? It doesn't take six months!*
> *It's a breakup – not a facelift."*
> Gabrielle on Desperate Housewives

Without presuming to label these celebrities specifically, all Oranges value their skill of quick decision-making. It is true that Oranges will be wildly successful at most anything they want. In their careers, on stage, or in front of the camera, they are usually right, and come out as winners. However, in those situations, Oranges are in control and accountable only to themselves.

Making relationship decisions with that same mindset comes with greater risks and smaller odds. A total belief that they can be successful at anything is a double-edged sword. Without a doubt, that unwavering belief and personality trait has brought these people (whether Orange or not) to the pinnacle of their professions. On the other hand, many also mistakenly believe those same talents instantly make a relationship work. While divorce is forever, marriage and love are often measured more in weeks or months.

> *"Maybe God wants us to meet a few wrong people*
> *before meeting the right one. So that when we*
> *finally meet the right person, we will know*
> *how to be grateful for that gift."*
> Author unknown

On the opposite end of the scale, psychologists at the University of Texas have been studying relationships and the tools to successful marriages for over 15 years. An on-going study has been following 168 couples who have been married since 1981. One of the findings to the success of long-term relationships has proven to be the value of a slow and steady courtship. Slow and deliberate usually does win in the long term over the Hollywood-type romance.

How to Avoid an Intimate Relationship

A final thought comes from the Saskatoon Pastoral Institute Newsletter. It outlines ten steps to totally avoid an intimate relationship. Sad, but true, each Color is amply represented:

Don't talk – if you are forced to talk stick to small-talk and avoid discussing true feelings.

Never show your feelings – showing any emotions gives you away, thus they must be avoided.

Always be pleasant – especially if something's wrong – it's important to fool your partner.

Always win – don't compromise or it becomes a dangerous precedent to showing you care.

Always keep busy – it allows you to hide and send the clear message that work is more important than your relationship.

Always be right – among other things, it allows you to keep the upper hand and stay in control.

Never argue – or you might discover you are different, which would mean making allowances, adjustments, and compromises.

That could lead to letting your partner see who you really are, or know what you really feel.

Make your partner guess what you want – when they guess wrong, which they will often, you are able to tell them they really don't understand or love you.

Always look out for number one – after all, you are the one making all the sacrifices in the relationship.

Keep the TV on at all times – especially if you're talking. Best of all, nobody will even notice that you don't communicate.

Oh no! Are you trying to make the Orange staff
read the policy manuals again?

It's hard to tell from your expressions
how excited you are about this.

Chapter Nine

Colors at Work

*Success on the job is 15% technical skills and 85%
attitude and the ability to relate to other people.*
Carnegie Foundation Study

For most of us, work consumes a large part of our lives. Whether
we love our job or... well, not so much, we spend our days with
people we did not get to vote on hiring. And if the truth were known,
we work with some rather strange people. Sure, that might sound
cruel, but it's not as though most of us have not had that thought.

If opposites attract in relationships, that's not the case at work.
There, our first thoughts are generally: *"if everybody just did things our
way, we would get along a lot better and things would run a lot smoother."*
Yet, work is an area where we interact with dozens of people in our
departments, large numbers of customers, or perhaps hundreds of
coworkers in the company. New hires, transfers, promotions, and a
host of other events throw us together with people we don't know
that well, don't get to choose, and with whom we now spend close
to a third of our week.

Some of the people we work with are just hard to understand.
Many just don't think like us or talk like us, and have totally different
ideas of how to get things done. When we ask about their weekend,
they tell us, *"fine,"* and that's it. How hurtful it is to someone who really
cares and wants to know. Others share a long story and...well, many
people are just being polite in asking and never wanted a long story.

Some want to have fun all day long while others just keep their heads down and stay focused and always task-oriented.

Without the insights of Colors, those misunderstandings are often true, and quite common. How many people would avoid countless aggravation or stress if they only understood their team's Colors and the unique strengths each person contributes? How many managers could easily reduce their turnover and increase productivity with a basic understanding of personality types?

70% of people do not quit their job.
They quit their manager.
Gallop Poll

At work, our four Colors are like various pieces of a jigsaw puzzle. Each one is a different, yet integral and critical part. Every Color contributes their own communication methods and long lists of strengths and skills, which greatly contribute to any team or office. Like the example of a jigsaw puzzle, each person plays an important part in the life of their company. Our strength and success comes from combining our talents with others, because alone, we cannot be everything to everybody. When working together, we become unstoppable as it takes all four Colors and an entire team effort to be successful, with everyone pulling in the same direction.

Would a perfect football team consist of nothing but running backs? Would anyone bet on the five highest scoring forwards in hockey if they were on a team with only each other? No chance. Every team requires the talents of various positions each with different strengths. Powerful and successful teams are created when individuals and specialists are combined with the talents of others to truly make any team or company successful. Working together and in harmony with one another, we become powerful and unstoppable by bringing together the talents and skills of our four Colors.

Blues at Work

"If I can make that person happy or make
someone smile for five or 10 minutes a day,
I feel I have accomplished something."
E.D. – Nursing assistant

In any office or team, recognizing the Blues will always be easy. When they ask us how we are, they really do want to know, and will make the time to listen and ask open-ended questions to get to know us. People will always come ahead of paperwork and few things are nicer than feeling a genuine sense of family in the office.

Even when we hire a new staff member, within hours Blues will quickly get to know his or her partner's name, and whether he or she has kids and what school they attend. Building relationships by making people feel included and part of their team are natural Blue gifts. They just have an unwavering commitment to building long lasting relationships in meaningful and genuine ways.

Blues build strong loyalties and friendships no matter what their job description or title is. It is no wonder these gifts always have Blues looking for positions where they are able to work with others in a cooperative environment. Blues prefer to avoid competitive situations where someone will become a winner and others the losers. In an ideal Blue work world, everyone succeeds, and rewards or recognition are shared equally. Teamwork really does make the dream work. If that means going along to get along, it is almost always worth it.

In the work Blues are passionate about, a little piece of their heart goes into everything they do. Blues will take the extra few minutes with a client, or they will be the tellers with a candy dish and that big smile, asking every customer how they are. It might not seem big, but it is always genuine. The downside to giving from their hearts is that Blues can personalize criticism and feel very uncomfortable and stressed when conflict arises. Even two people clear across the office raising their voices have a noticeable impact on Blues. This creates the need to tread gently with constructive feedback or criticism, because we are speaking directly to their hearts. This is also one of the primary reasons why Blues look for bosses who make them feel valued, listen well, and understand their feelings.

Blues love the chance to verbalize their dreams and ideas where others will listen and respect their intuition and imagination. After all, they are the big-picture visionaries, and this respect will greatly build their enthusiasm and energy. They look for these same values in meetings where everyone has the chance to share their ideas in a safe environment.

Denise is a Blue department manager in a large corporation. Without telling anyone, her boss had planned a staff conference as a two-part meeting. At the conclusion of the first portion, her boss simply asked Denise and two other staff members to leave. Only another Blue person could understand how hurtful and embarrassing that was. Without explanation, and in a matter-of-fact way, she felt like she was being excluded from the group.

Her first reaction was to use humor to deflect from her true feelings. Once outside the boardroom, this quickly turned to anger and frustration, followed by a good cry. Yet very few people even noticed what happened. When two staff members who understood a little about Denise's personality offered her a hug, she actually refused. The great Blue sense of intuition, and ability to spot a phony, clearly saw that this was more patronizing than real.

Golds at Work

"When I find something that works, I stick with it."
Dan Reeves

From their childhood in scouts to company presidents, Golds believe in always being prepared. It is in the DNA of their Color and as critical as oxygen is for breathing. They perform best when jobs, tasks, reports, meetings, and the majority of their lives at work are properly planned and on-track. Golds are at their most efficient when they are able to work pro-actively and know what will be coming at them – today and next week.

As natural rule-followers, Golds look for clear directions and specific goals. Few things make Golds more nervous than vague instructions or exceptions. They prefer fixed, black and white rules. Any vagueness can leave Golds guessing and stressing whether they are on track, or doing the right things the right way. Once they have the framework and details, a job gets done, done on time, and done accurately. There are no excuses or delays, as Golds have very high standards for themselves and expect the same quality work from others.

Their work ethic makes Golds some of the hardest working people. While they are in their work mode, however, Golds do not have much time for socializing or stopping to smell the roses. Right now there is a job to be done before they can relax. As great team players, they will always be helpful and supportive in picking up the slack, covering for their team, or going way above and beyond what is expected.

Without fanfare or seeking attention, Golds do their job because it needs doing. Their motto is generally that *if it needs to be – it's up to me*. With their strong sense of loyalty and duty, Golds can seem to take the workload and stress of the entire office onto their shoulders. It is why they love to receive a thank-you and a little recognition. Yet, Golds will downplay this as unnecessary and minimize the attention as *they are just doing their job.* Do not let that fool us. Tangible recognition, such as a certificate, gift card, or something practical for their desks goes a very long way with Golds who will never forget it.

Tried, tested, and true might be an old Ford slogan, but it certainly fits Golds just as well. Golds usually take the same routes to work, default to the same places for lunch, and have set routines of cleaning up their desks and making tomorrow's to-do lists before going home. And where an Orange may view this as boring, it is simply a Gold's comfort zone and where they function best. Why reinvent the wheel? Routines allow for efficiencies where no details get missed, and become the most logical way to get things done. Changing procedures, job descriptions, or major portions of their routine can be stressful to Golds. Their resistance to change, or natural defense of *"we've always done it that way,"* is often a fear of the unknown, or a worry that new procedures may not be as efficient.

Golds accomplish their work in a systematic and organized manner. First, they just need to clean up their desks and finish off a few loose ends. After that, Golds can concentrate and get to work. Once they get started, Golds expect to be trusted to get their jobs done without follow-up or being micro-managed. As a result, Golds find great comfort in routines and structure, because both ensure they do not have to keep asking questions or wasting time by getting off track. Once the most effective "how-to" template is in place, Golds would really love *that* to be their fixed routine for a very long time.

Lori is a finance manager for a car dealership. She is a Gold working in the high Orange environment of the automotive industry. This involves significant and continuous multi-

tasking, constant interruptions, sales people with "just a quick question" in and out of her office, and a need to be totally flexible in any sales approach. Lori has at least a dozen possible buyers to work with at any one time and finds it impossible to control her day or stick to any to-do list.

She rarely takes a day off and can always be counted on to help other staff and departments and always goes the extra mile without being asked. Her income is six figures – who wouldn't want that pay? But the job is quickly burning her out and her stress has started to manifest itself in a number of physical ways already.

Lori is a Gold caught up in a stressful catch-22. Her Gold wants the great pay, while her very Gold boss allows Lori a fair degree of freedom on most days and micro-manages her on others. Lori hates the scrambling each day and changes of any kind, especially when thinking about switching jobs. Yet every day she longs to work in a structured and pro-active job where she can plan her work in advance and know what tomorrow will bring. She craves an environment where she is recognized and valued in ways that cannot simply be measured by looking at her commission check each month.

Oranges at Work

Sir Richard Branson's Rules of Business:

Keep it casual	Haggle: Everything's negotiable
Have fun working	Move like a bullet
Smile	Don't lead sheep or herd cats
Size does matter	Be a common, regular person

Would every person not love to have a career where work does not seem like work at all? Who would not love going to work with enthusiasm, total flexibility, and looking forward to each day as a new adventure? Well, almost every Orange person does. Yet these strengths can be badly and wrongly labeled and misinterpreted by coworkers and bosses who do not understand what makes Oranges stay motivated or engaged – those things that have them wanting to come to work in the first place.

Oranges are the energy in any company with their infectious can-do positive attitude and continual sense of humor. They seem to be in perpetual motion with their endless energy. Often the last place to look for an Orange is at their desks. This is why they tend to gravitate towards jobs which have a fair amount of freedom to move around. Oranges will definitely spend a lot of effort avoiding being cooped up in an office, or stuck in a world of predictability and routines.

They look for positions which offer freedom and excitement in a high-energy, competitive environment, without a lot of unnecessary structure. They are the risk-takers of the world with a high level of self-confidence. Oranges are also the largest number of entrepreneurs who readily jump first and figure out their plans on the way down.

It is no wonder that Oranges are the biggest group of employees in a wide range of sales positions, since these careers have more freedom, fewer rules, less routines, and limited paperwork. These sales-based jobs are also a chance to be paid for success – with bonuses, awards, or contests. After all, most sales positions have little or no base salary, *so we eat what we kill when we are out in the real world making things happen* – whatever it takes not to punch a time clock.

With their great networking skills, Oranges know everybody, and almost everybody likes them. In the office, others act as Orange's go-to people when they are stuck, or need some quick help, because Oranges likely have not read any of the manuals or latest updates. When something needs to get done, or when a client is waiting, *that* is not the time to find the policy manual. Besides, they would rather ask for forgiveness than permission. Oranges act and learn in a hands-on, trial and error manner. Training them for a new position should take a day or two, tops. After that, they want to jump in with both feet and figure out the rest of what they need to learn as they go along.

In meetings or anything away from the real world of work, Oranges can become quite impatient. They are not interested in sitting around talking about issues when there is real work to be done. No meeting should ever last more than 30 minutes, tops. Oranges just want to make a decision, any decision, because it can always be changed tomorrow if a better idea comes along. Next week counts as long-term planning, and that seems like an eternity from now.

Spend just a few minutes in any television studio or radio station and you quickly notice the vast numbers of Oranges and Blues. Both Colors have great flexibility, which is a crucial strength in the media business, and both Colors thrive by working with (or helping) people.

Recently a radio station installed a new integrated telephone and computer system. There was nobody around who knew how the system really worked that first day when Linda started her regular talk show. Yet, her first words were, "OK, this could be fun…" and she actually meant it!

No, the phones didn't work after the first call, or pretty much throughout the show. It's a good thing Oranges are great multi-taskers. As Linda continued talking on the air, she unplugged a couple of things, pressed this and that, re-booted the computer, and quickly hit the mute button to ask her producer to find the tech guy, while continuing to interview her guest on the air.

In between, she took a call on her cell phone to pass on some question and never became stressed. It really was a game to win, or a challenge to overcome, but never affected the tone of her voice, her demeanor, or the quality of her show.

During the second hour it got worse when the scheduled guest never did show up. No problem – stuff happens. Instead, Linda went to the organization's web site and talked for 15 minutes on their upcoming theatre production with zero notice, yet no hesitation. For two hours, Linda never stumbled, or gave her huge audience any clues that her planned segment and her entire show had totally come unglued. Whatever the industry or job, that takes talent and you can count on an Orange to pull it off with ease.

Greens at Work

"Of course I know the answer, but I'm not sure I can communicate it in ways your listeners would understand."
Economics professor responding to an interview question

Greens are intelligent and they know it. It is something they continue to earn with their never-ending love of learning and special gifts of problem solving and lateral thinking. Greens are continually probing, questioning, or challenging the status-quo, and never settle for the easy answers. The more complex the challenge, the higher a Green's motivation level to finding a solution, improving a process, or perhaps developing a better strategy.

Few things are more satisfying than having the entire office panicked and stressed out before stepping in to solve the problem. If their Orange coworkers enjoy team sports, problem solving is the Green equivalent. It is not done for the recognition, but for the internal satisfaction, often against all odds, when everyone else has given up, and a number of possible solutions have been missed.

Doing anything right and doing it the right way, however, does not come instantly but, it is always worth the time and effort. From projects to reports, presentations to decision-making, good enough is never good enough. It started way back in school where a mark of 80 was not a reason to celebrate, but rather to focus on the 20 percent they got wrong, in order to improve. When Greens do commit to a decision, others can always rely on it. After that, information stands until better information comes along. It is also why Greens have a special disdain for being asked to re-work a report or project.

Greens are gifted strategists and long-term thinkers who prefer to work pro-actively, instead of scrambling to make re-active decisions. They perform best when seeing the big picture and overall logic, and prefer to work alone to structure their work in their own fashion and on their own terms. Two must-have tools for Greens are books and computers. After all, knowledge is power and information is king. Greens love technology, gadgets, and their computers. In fact, the I.T. and computer fields are magnets for Greens who enjoy working with others who share their approach to problem solving in a logical manner.

"(At PayPal) you didn't measure where you were in the
organization by how many people you're managing.
Prestige was measured by how few people
there were above you who could prevent
you from doing what you wanted to do."
David Sacks, former COO in
Fortune Magazine interview

Greens place a huge emphasis on credibility. It applies to their performance standards and decision-making processes just as much as their judgments of others. If someone, anyone, has a better way, any

Green would love to discuss the issue. They could certainly be wrong or find a better way – being wrong is how they get to be right! But the person had better come prepared to substantiate their arguments based on facts and concrete evidence. Greens do not take being questioned as an insult, but rather as an opportunity to debate and perhaps learn something along the way. Just do not expect Greens to go along simply to get along.

While their consistently calm, cool, and collected demeanor is great for poker games, it can make Greens hard to get to know, or even to understand what is really going on in their minds. Where their Blue coworkers feel and share someone's pain, Greens understand it, instead. Emotional displays are seen as a weakness and public displays of affection make Greens quite uncomfortable. Even excessive social situations, or anything beyond a couple of sentences of small talk, is generally avoided at all cost.

Find the Job You Love

Do what you love to do and
you'll never have to work again!

Do someone's Colors have an affect on their job and career choices? Can all of us really do any job we want? The answer to both is yes – but…

Studies show that the average person will make at least four or five different career choices throughout their working life. Hopefully, each of these will bring someone closer to their dream job – one that not only pays well (the reality of life), but also a job which fits their preferences and ideal work environment, as well as their Colors. Yes, any person can do any job. However, if their personality is not a fit for the job, it can become a question of how long they may actually stay.

Most people look for the big picture in a career, not a pigeonholed job description matched to a Color. The emphasis is more about the overall job, the work environment, the larger corporate culture, the type (and Colors) of a boss, and how the position interacts with others. All of these factors contribute to creating the right fit.

Different Colors are naturally better suited for certain jobs and tasks, but talents and skills come in all Colors. People just require higher amounts of dedication, concentration, and discipline when a job is not a natural fit. Anyone can do the job, but it often requires more energy and effort than a career which matches someone's personality more closely. Part of that may explain why less than 20 percent of college and university graduates are still in the career of their degree ten years later. People really can do almost anything they put their minds to, but will it make them happy? Will it create a sense of self-satisfaction or build their self-esteem?

We make a living by what we do
and a life by who we are.

Can a Blue person be a really good file clerk? You bet! Talent, skills, and I.Q. have nothing to do with Colors. But will they stay for any length of time in a position that probably has no interaction with others? Not likely, since one of the most important values for Blues is teamwork. Most Blues would feel punished working in isolation from their team, whereas Greens really enjoy having their own space and the chance to work independently. Can an Orange work strictly at a desk job with no chance to move around, following fixed rules and strict procedures? Of course! Will they still be in the job a year from now? Don't bet on it.

At some time or another, the core values of someone's Colors will come to the surface in their work or career choices. But then, it is reasonably easy for most us to make some small changes in our job to be able to do more of what we value, and less of what we don't, without having to change careers, jobs, or companies.

Karen has been a divorce lawyer all of her career. Yet, as a Blue, she was never comfortable or fulfilled in a career that was often adversarial and confrontational. What hurt Karen the most was the effect of an ugly divorce fight on the children. She always felt as though she was somehow contributing to the conflict, fighting, and scars on the children.

As a result, Karen changed her entire law office to the practice of wills and estates. While it was a lot more procedural and paperwork-related, at least she was away from the frequent confrontation and hateful exchanges between ex spouses spending tons of money and energy wanting to be right way more than being happy.

In the last number of years, however, more and more emphasis in divorce law has evolved towards mediation and counseling. Today, Karen has returned to handling divorce law, but through mediation and not litigation. The first question she now asks her potential clients is whether they are looking to make their divorce into a win-win for their children or whether they are determined to take their spouse to court. The former, Karen will help – the latter she refers to someone else. With the changes in the divorce laws she is now able to go from a "conflict" lawyer to a helping, counseling, mediation, and win-win lawyer while staying in her chosen career.

What Each Color Wants to Ask and Find

Can any company create the perfect environment or workplace for every Color? Not likely – and probably unnecessary. In fact, our skills and talents have no connection to our work environments, but have more to do with our productivity and comfort zones.

Each Color has their unique strengths, stresses, and work preferences. As a result, each person looks for certain *want to have* and *need to have* aspects of their position. This drive often begins with the type of questions someone asks during their initial job interview. It also tends to continue throughout many people's careers in looking to shape any work environment to fit the comfort zone of their Colors. Every day, employers look to recruit ideal staff as employees search for their dream jobs. For most companies, a minor change in the office or in someone's job description creates a measurable payoff in employee satisfaction, reduced turnover, and productive teamwork. After all, teamwork is less about the ability to work together, but much more about the willingness to do so.

Strange, but true, that the average company spends less than 2% of their training budget on front-line staff. Yet these are the employees who almost single-handedly control sales volume, customer satisfaction, and repeat business.

Blues seek to know:

- Does the company listen to me and my needs and do they really care?

- Is there a teamwork-type approach to work and a creative, positive environment, or am I on my own?

- Do I feel valued, included, and can I make a difference?

- Are we doing anything together away from work such as social functions, team building, etc. where we get to know each other and develop our relationships?

- Will I have assistance for conflict and problem resolution?

- Is my boss someone who listens well and respects my feelings and those of my teammates?

- Do I get to use my people skills with clients and staff, or is my workday purely task-oriented?

My ideal workplace promotes and encourages teamwork and open interaction with others. I seek a chance to be involved in the decision-making and the opportunity to verbalize ideas with my team. I treat others as members of my extended family, not just fellow employees. I love working with people that have strong listening skills, respect my opinions, and take me seriously. I am awesome at getting everyone involved and making them feel included. I look for coworkers who share my strengths of verbal communication and flexibility and a company that is sensitive to the effect of corporate change on their staff. I look for a workplace that values my contributions in customer service and teamwork, and not only in terms of quantity of work.

Golds seek to know:

- Will you trust me to do the job, letting me be in charge of getting things done, and setting up my own routines and scheduling?

- Am I going to have a sense of belonging here?

- When taking on extra work, do you ask me or tell me?

- Is this a stable company, branch, department and management, or will there be a lot of stress with transfers, turnover, changes in policies, etc.

- Do you recognize staff for their contributions in fair, measurable, and tangible ways?

- Will I have clear and consistent instructions, rules, expectations, stability, and time-lines?

My ideal workplace is well laid out and organized, with clear rules and expectations that are enforced fairly for everyone. I enjoy having my own space and the chance to put up my awards and certificates and stay organized. I look for managers that recognize my ability to complete any assignment without follow-up or excuses, and who reward my work regularly and fairly. I value consistent operating standards with fixed and predictable routines and procedures with minimal stress or conflict. I look for a workplace that respects my scheduling ability and allows me to work on things that need to be done today, one thing at a time, and without excessive interruptions or last-minute changes.

Oranges seek to know:

- Are there enough new challenges, problems to solve, hands-on work, and variety every day?

- Is it a fun, positive, and energetic environment? Can I move around or am I stuck at my desk?

- How hung up is the company on rules and fixed procedures? Is there some flexibility on deadlines and in how to get my work done?

- How much of the job is people and customer work versus paperwork?

- If I can handle six things at once, is there teamwork to help me finish the details and paperwork?

My idea of a great workplace is one which has very little structure, rules, or routines. I look for freedom and the chance to get hands-on involvement to make things happen with my creativity and my need for action. I don't want to talk about it or have a meeting – I want to get on with it – hands on, right now. I look for a boss that appreciates my high energy, multi-tasking skills, and problem-solving strengths. My company should reward me in real and tangible ways and give me direct and straightforward instructions without too much detail or big picture stuff. I love to be let loose on any challenge and I work well under stress if I am given the freedom to do my thing.

Greens seek to know:

- Am I allowed sufficient independent work time?

- How much of the position is re-active versus pro-active? Will I have the time to do it right, instead of right now?

- Is this a progressive company willing to invest in new technology, software, and training to keep us current?

- Will I have the tools and resources to do my job in the most effective manner?

- If and when I have feedback and suggestions for improvements, will management listen to me?

- Can I contribute to teaching others and also keep learning, upgrading, and asking questions?

My ideal workplace has wide-open but a low noise area. I look for the chance to have quiet periods of thinking time without interruption or distractions. I want to emulate the structure used by teams of researchers, where there is extensive interaction with others that share my creativity and logic. I love opportunities to discuss and debate complex problems, to have a chance to share my knowledge and research. I value a manager that is not pushy or in need of instant answers to complex questions and a company that values doing anything and everything right the first time, every time. I look for someone who recognizes my strengths of research and innovation, of contributing to the big picture of the department.

It's Not Always About Money

Successful companies foster an environment and culture which truly cares and values their staff. In return, employees increasingly care about their clients, profitability, and the growth of their company. Meeting those challenges and doing it well pays off through productivity growth, increased profits, reduced turnover, measurable teamwork, and satisfied repeat customers.

> *Talent and success in any career comes wrapped*
> *in all shapes, sizes, and Colors. It is not the color*
> *of the wrapping, but the talent of the person*
> *which is important.*

The companies who do this well are frequently featured in magazines and top 50-type lists. However, since a vast majority of businesses employ less than 100 staff, the power of creating successful and well-functioning teams applies just as much to millions of small and medium sized firms. With smaller offices, less bureaucracy, and fewer management levels, it also becomes much easier to create.

One of the best examples of living the understanding and power of Colors and team building is Paull Travel in Edmonton, Alberta. The owner, Lesley Paull, is a strong Orange. What could be more perfect than a career which allows for extensive travel, a wide variety of tasks, and constant interactions with people, all within an industry fraught with constant challenges and changes? Paull continually uses her knowledge of personality types to build her teams around their Colors, selling skills, strengths, and workplace preferences in order to align job descriptions with their Colors. *"I even had some team members who were just not totally comfortable with selling. So I realigned my staff to make that possible."*

Today, her staff actually consists of half travel agents and half support staff – something unheard of in the industry, and judged as totally impossible by almost all her peers. It is a good thing Orange business-owners do not make decisions based on the tried and tested methods, or traditional organizational structures.

Radical as this approach may seem, Paull Travel continues to enjoy unparalleled growth through some of the most difficult and challenging times in the industry. Her Orange staff can excel at their strengths without the stress or "punishment" of excessive paperwork. Her Gold staff does contribute to travel sales, but focus primarily on a team-approach with an Orange partner-agent and take responsibility for handling the details, planning, and paperwork. In fact, Paull has a number of agents whose individual volume exceeds that of an average travel agency! At the end of the day, results speak louder than words, truly a great motto for any Orange.

At the same time, Paull's definition of support staff is not a typical one. All incentives, bonuses, training, gifts, and trips include her entire team, regardless of job description or title. *"We always do everything together. We don't have two different classes of staff – ever,"* says Paull. In fact, bonuses can sometimes be a significant part of the support staff's pay. *"I don't judge people on just one scale. Whether they are support or selling agents, they are all equally important."*

Unlike corporate sales, travel agents utilize very different skill sets. Corporate sales are significantly more organized and straightforward while leisure travel requires significantly more time and creativity. Both are major differences Paull is very aware of. Her office functions efficiently and as a team. Business is great, stress is at a minimum, and job functions are geared to utilize everyone's natural talents. How much turnover would she have without using these tools? While she modestly deflects the question, the answer is clear.

Paull relates a typical story that many Oranges love, and hear often. One of her largest clients had changed travel agents for a minor discount with a competitor. It did not take long before he returned, sharing that *"they didn't know who I was and never made me laugh."* These are powerful words frequently heard by Oranges with their high-energy, great enthusiasm, and constant personal touch and attention. It is clearly one of the keys to the continued growth of her business, which is frequently unknown, overlooked, or underrated by others.

> *"You'll never (really) get people to work for you,*
> *but you can get people to work with you."*
> Murray Koffler, Founder: Shoppers Drug Mart

What's family planning, Mom? I'm the only Gold
in our family so I should probably be in charge of that.

I've been grounded so often, I taught myself how to play the guitar.
Next week I start a 5 city tour — is that cool or what?

Chapter Ten

The Colors of Children: Doing More of What Works

*Don't treat all your kids the same. Treat
them all fairly, but in the unique ways
which matter to their Colors.*

Almost everyone who is blessed enough to have children of their own remembers that frustrated comment from their parents growing up: *"Wait until you have kids!"* Well, that parental threat wouldn't be such a challenge if our kids turned out to be like us. If so, we would have a template of what to expect, and an idea of where and at what age challenges with our own children might arise.

Unfortunately, there are no outside influences which determine the personality types of newborns. This virtually assures that every family will be a rainbow of Colors. Two spouses of different Colors, along with one or more children, each with their own Color combinations creates a colorful home. Those differences likely assure that every parent has at least one child who totally prevents him or her from ever writing a book on how to parent.

From the state of their room, to learning styles, to differing communication preferences, children show their personality types pretty clearly, and at very early ages. A few clues to their Colors can already be seen in babies where some seem to enjoy more quiet time and space, or never fuss much after waking up. Perhaps there are many Blue clues when babies thrive on a lot of extra physical touch. Some are quiet and easygoing, while others are more restless and perpetually on the move.

At an early age, children will also start to dream about a variety of different career choices. Quite often, many values of their Colors can influence their passions and ideas. A great example is singer Alanis Morissette. Before the age of eight, a family friend took her along to a concert. It turned out to be Morissette's first realization that it was possible to make a living singing and entertaining. In her words, *"you can love what you do – this is exciting."* Long before she became a teenager, Morissette had scrapbooks full of songs, appeared on children's television shows, and even recorded her first single.

Just as insightful was an interview with the father of a teenager from Winnipeg who already holds a number of cancer research patents: *"I knew my son was different in grade seven when he didn't want to go play, but just wanted to read and do research."*

Until their mid-teens, the majority of children exhibit many Orange behaviors, even if that is not their primary Color. A high energy level, the inability to sit still, and testing the rules and boundaries, are general Orange behaviors all children share to some degree. At the same time as they seek ways to be individuals, children also have a strong need for belonging, which is one of the key motivators for children of all ages. However, it is not difficult to discover their actual Colors simply by watching any child at play, with their friends, under stress, or doing their homework.

Children themselves already know the basic descriptors of Colors in their own language. At school age, the basic labeling simply tends to be nerd, class clown, teacher's pet, or wimp, to name a few. In later years, teenagers become some of the biggest fans of Colors since its tools create many insights to understanding the behaviors of their siblings, parents, teachers, and friends. Colors provides children with simple and practical ways to express themselves. It puts words to their feelings and stresses, and gives them a greater insight and appreciation of the high Gold school structure.

Colors also provide a framework for children to discover that it is okay to be unique and different from others. Peer pressure, parenting styles, and a range of teachers and friends with varying priorities, make today's world a huge minefield for children and teenagers to maneuver.

For parents, these tools create many insights, not hindsight, into the special qualities of their children. Understanding Colors within a family reduces the chance of subconsciously attempting to mold a child to match a parent's personality type. It reduces frustration and confusion in wondering why they seem to have such a different set of values or stresses. After all, children are not mini-adults and will continue to grow into their own unique personality types.

The most powerful A's your children want don't come from the school system. They are your approval, admiration, accolades, applause, and attention.

The basic needs and wants for children are the same as those of their parents. Children need to know each parent is 100 percent there for them. In the same way adults relate to others at work, children need and deserve that same undivided attention at home. When we are at home, are we really there? Are we engaged? Are we mentally, spiritually, and physically there for them? Just as communication styles are different between adults, they are also very different for children and need to be adapted into the language of the child, to their Color, and not to the communication preference of the adult or parent's Colors.

Talking to children without understanding the language, values, and stresses of their Colors can create distance and foster the feeling of a real generation gap. On the other hand, being attuned to their Colors becomes a powerful tool for growing and strengthening each relationship and serves as a significant building block for their self-esteem. For children, it is never the size of the paycheck, or the big problems of the work-world, but rather all the little things that impact their lives in powerful and lasting ways.

When you become aware of your child's Colors,
you are able to encourage and support them in
their dreams, instead of fitting them into yours.

Blue Children

At an early age, a Blue child is already quite emotional and sensitive. Parents will quickly notice the signs that their sons or daughters always wear their hearts on their sleeves and can get their feelings hurt easily. These children value helping others, building a large circle of friends, and looking to ensure everyone is happy and included. These life-long gifts may also contribute to developing an early Blue trait of bending to the wishes of others, and being quite susceptible to peer-pressure and bullies.

In a new school or neighborhood, Blue children will make friends quite quickly and easily. Their open demeanor, willingness to share, and gifts for making others feel special, naturally attracts friends. At any age, they make the effort to be the peacemakers, or to smooth things over whenever possible. Yes, Blue feelings already run very deep. They value the physical touch and hugs, and they need others to really listen, without cutting them off, or making fun of them.

Blue children communicate in a very animated manner and look for positive reassurances, always seeking to feel included and to be liked. Negativity or criticism affects them deeply and is often confused with failure. Just a simple sharp comment from one of their friends or teachers can have negative effects which may linger for a long time.

These children look for group environments and cooperative learning situations where lessons are adaptable to individual needs. They are not interested in processes or procedures as much as they are interested in their friends and the other kids around them. Stories, interactive games, and sensory-oriented activities, are the easiest ways for Blues to learn. In school, they tend to love classes involving social studies, music, and drama. And, they prefer any projects or homework which they can complete as a team and with their friends.

One group of Blue children who will have a more difficult time in school and with their friends is Blue boys. As one of the smallest Color groups, they can spend a lifetime wondering why they seem to be so different. These Blue boys are much less competitive, more caring, more compassionate, and significantly more feelings-oriented than other boys. Even at home, when parents do not understand the insights of Colors, Blue boys may receive feedback such as, *"don't cry"* or *"don't be so sensitive."* As a result, many retreat into a mask of their second Color. This mask, almost like their game-face, helps Blue boys hide their sensitivities and emotions until they feel it is safe to let others see them for who they really are.

> *"I would travel to every country in the world*
> *and tell people to love each other."*
> Grade six students' answer to: What would
> you give the world as a Christmas present?

Blue Learning Styles

Every Blue child would love to start their day with a hug. At school, their drive for meaningful relationships grows when learning is done in group settings and team activities. They seek to make learning and school into a group journey involving frequent opportunities to share and to interact with others. Working together and sharing with others builds their self-esteem and enhances their abilities and enjoyment of learning. Imposed deadlines help them to stay on task, as does the possibility of being separated from their group should they not stay focused. Blue children enjoy contributing and helping others and love the chance to be helpful to their team, instructor, and friends.

Blue children value an overview and outline before getting into detailed modules or segments. Learning only in pieces or sections without understanding the big picture can be challenging. In those cases, or in working with extensive abstract material, a Blue child can easily get sidetracked, or start to daydream.

Naturally, Blue children thrive with Blue teachers or instructors who are attuned to their needs and desires, which include the foundation of receiving individual and personal attention. Fortunately, that actually happens in most cases, as the majority of elementary school, pre-school, and daycare staff also tend to be Blues.

In the school system, it will be up to parents to communicate feedback to teachers. Blue children will not likely stand up for their needs, or acknowledge when their feelings have been hurt. It will only be at home, with their parents, where Blues will supply honest and more direct feedback. Being aware that Blue children have a real challenge standing up for their needs, it is helpful for teachers to watch that Blues do not succumb to peer pressure. Teachers must assure that these children do get a chance to develop their own opinions and are heard, without feeling judged or laughed at.

Gold Children

It will not take long for a Gold child to develop a strong drive for responsibility and a keen sense of right and wrong. In their early teens, Golds can already seem to be mini-adults, and be more disciplined in getting their homework done before allowing themselves to have fun. Gold kids will likely have a room that is certainly neater than most of their peers, and value earning an allowance by completing their chores. Often, these will also be the kids who save quite a bit of their money, or think and plan carefully before spending much of it.

They are quite comfortable in the background and behind the scenes, instead of being the center of attention. At home, Gold children look for stability, the safety of fixed routines, and discipline which is fair and consistent. They gain self-esteem (and probably their allowance) by being helpful and contributing around the house.

A Gold child starts at an early age to be quite comfortable with fixed rules. The good news is that this is the least likely Color to skip school more than a few times a year, because they actually worry about getting caught. Knowing they are breaking the rules takes much of the fun out of it in the first place. This attitude also contributes to making most Gold children the teacher's pet in school. Teachers certainly love kids who tend to sit still, pay attention, and do their homework without excessive prompting.

Gold children love to have their own room, or at least their own closet or separate personal space somewhere in the house. It allows them to organize their toys, desk, and dresser their own way, and to feel a strong sense of structure and order. At almost any age, this contributes to building their sense of self-esteem and helps them to relax. Unfortunately, it is not something which is shared by their brothers or sisters of any other Color which often leads to needless stress and conflict – and a big reason to be careful with whom Gold children share a room.

I'm a high Orange married to a Green and our baby, who is three, is definitely Gold! This has been pretty prominent for quite a while – it just took learning about Colors to figure it out. Every toy in his room has a place, he keeps a few toys on show (which don't get touched until he changes them), his desk is empty unless he's using it, and my son has a schedule for himself that doesn't change.

The other day my son and his cousin were playing in his room – they usually play in his brother's room. It's OK to mess up his room: we get to play AND my room stays neat! When it was time to leave, I didn't check to see if the kids needed to clean up. Usually they don't make a big mess so I wasn't worried. We got into the truck and my son started in on me that my truck was "filthy" (his word). So to make him happy, we went through the car wash. (As a result, I forgot about half the things on my Orange sort-of to-do list.)

That night, I walked into his room, and it was as messy as his brother's! Every toy, book and crayon was on the floor. I told my son he'd have to clean it in the morning, as I cleared a path to his bed. About 20 minutes later we heard noises from his room – which isn't like him to play after the lights go out. My husband put him back to bed, but this happened about three times before he actually went to sleep.

The next morning when I went into his room, it was spotless. Everything was back in its place! A little while later my son came to me and told me that he was sorry he wasn't sleeping last night, but it "bugged him" that his room was messy. He just couldn't sleep without cleaning up first. This happens at school also. The one activity for his playschool the other day was to cut out a paper star. Everyone in his class cut the paper into a million little pieces and went on to something else. His actually looked like a star – but he was still upset that he went off the lines. When he colors, it's the same thing!

Of course, we don't mess with his schedule too much, if we can avoid it. Before the last school break my husband volunteered to take the boys to school. Well I guess Daddy didn't do things 'right,' because his whole day was a little off, and after that he was still quite agitated when I picked him up. Since the Colors seminar we definitely parent differently. The kids have different punishments now, and the way we interact with them has grown a lot! – M.W.

At home and at school, Gold children look for specific and detailed instructions. They need lesson plans and tasks which follow a logical outline and include books and resource materials. Among their favorite subjects are band and language arts classes, along with subjects that have right or wrong answers, such as math.

> *"The police in a small town in Florida actually received a phone call from a seven-year old wanting to report that he caught his grandfather cheating at cards."*

Gold Learning Styles

The Gold need for structure and stable routines naturally extends to the education system. But then, most learning environments are already designed in a Gold manner, with fixed rules, agendas, and report cards to measure and evaluate progress. This framework allows a Gold child to focus on his or her natural drive to stay task-oriented.

Gold children, just like Gold adults, look for proper structure and systems, along with clear and detailed instructions. They value their ability to stay on track and are frequently turned off by others who get sidetracked, joke around too much, or wander off topic. These behaviors can noticeably detract from their learning experiences since Gold children generally have no difficulty staying focused and conforming to acceptable behaviors.

Gold children look for logical lesson plans and agendas which include specific steps. They value being graded along the way. Since they want to assure they stay on track, Golds need checkpoints, feedback, and report cards which measure their progress and help them feel a sense of tangible accomplishment.

They tend to have the same high expectations of their instructors as they do of themselves. Generally, with a constant concern about their marks, Gold children will be harder on themselves than any teacher or instructor will be. Their mindset focuses on an overall desire to get the job done and done right. Even as younger kids, Golds can seem to have a business-like approach to learning, which greatly appeals to their orderly nature. However, it is also critical for Gold children to learn the life-long lessons that good enough sometimes really is good enough, and that it is also OK to have fun along the way.

My very organized fourth grade daughter's homework comes home every Monday and is due back Friday morning. When this started, I was "helping" her organize what she would do each day by labeling tasks with color coded Post-It notes. Being rather Orange, I had her do a little vocabulary work, a little math, then a little reading each day throughout the week, because this variety and changing things up seemed more fun to me.

We seemed to spend hours doing homework and at least once a week we both had stressed-out tears, and I was often at a loss of how to be more helpful. It was dreadful, to put it mildly! About a week after I got home from my first Colors seminar, she asked if she could color code what she wanted to do each day. I was looking for anything that would help and readily agreed. I was surprised to see her color code her homework completely differently than I had been doing.

She chose one subject to do from start to finish each day. So, Monday was math, Tuesday was vocabulary, etc. The even more amazing thing is that she gets her homework done in a small fraction of the time it used to take, and with very little stress! All I could think about was, wow, Orange mommy, Gold kid! Thank you so much for opening my eyes to her Colors and how I can best respect when to step in and, more difficult for me, when to let her do her thing.   – S.W.

Orange Children

If all children have an endless amount of energy, parents can double that with an Orange child. While trying anything and everything, pushing boundaries, and bending the rules, Orange kids will have fun and enjoy the social part of life – for life. They make friends easily, love physical activities, hate to lose, and almost always have a room that looks like it has been hit by a tornado.

One of the greatest appeals for Orange children is the stimulation of interacting with others – any social scene will do. They do not handle boredom well and do whatever it takes to have or create a little excitement, if not always in positive ways. From the time they first interact with other kids on the playground, Orange children become the natural leaders among their friends. And, as natural performers, they thrive on attention and action which greatly enhances their self-esteem.

Too much structure, fixed routines, and too many rules are a big turn-off to Orange children. Parents also learn quickly that their Orange child is not keen on too much talk or theory. *"Let me at it – let's see what I can do"* is their general motto. Just doing it is always their preferred approach, instead of following instructions that teach theory, rules, or structure.

Throughout their lives, Oranges value hands-on experiences. Ideally, they do not want to be penalized for attempts, but only for the final results. An easy example is putting together a gift or toy. There is very little chance any Orange (child or adult) will pull out the instructions. Instead, they will take the parts and start putting them together through trial and error. Only after they are finished and can see the final results, do the instructions make sense.

It is no wonder Orange children are often misjudged or misunderstood. This may be part of the reason that the numbers of children diagnosed with Attention-Deficit/Hyperactivity Disorder (ADHD) has grown in huge numbers over the past few years. Today, the U.S. Food and Drug Administration estimates that more than 2.5 million children take stimulant medication for ADHD.

It does not take much imagination to guess that the vast majority of these kids are Orange. And, boys are diagnosed with ADHD three times more than girls. As discussed in the Orange chapter, it is not a question of the legitimacy of ADHD, but it does warrant asking if drugs may be attempting to medicate a personality type. After all, labels last a lifetime, and quick *fixes* can sometimes do more harm than good. In fact, the American Heart Association has now begun calling for heart testing prior to prescribing any ADHD medication due to possible side affects on heart rates and blood pressure.

Over the past few years, more and more studies have also investigated the possible links between antidepressant drugs and violent behavior. In the words of author Mike Adams, who has reported extensively that many of these drugs have never been tested on children, nor approved by the FDA for use with children, "*If you're going to alter the brain chemistry of these children you had better be prepared for the results.*" It is precisely why the United Kingdom has instituted a total ban on these medications for children.

Macleans magazine recently published an entire feature story entitled, "*The Legal Drugging of School Kids.*" In a letter to the editor, a doctor asked why we would rather take an opinion from someone with a white coat than taking responsibility into our own hands by altering our kid's poor diet with sugar-loaded soft drinks, and feeding them better? In his opinion, the answer is simple: "*We have been manipulated into believing that getting control of our children is just one pill away.*" Without minimizing the seriousness of a valid diagnosis, psychologists agree that there are many other avenues to try before considering medication. One of the most effective is a yoga class, and either dance, art, or music. In addition, a serious focus should be placed on drastically reducing the intake of sugar. (For some further insights, google Mike Adams and/or go to naturalnews.com)

Orange Learning Styles

Since learning styles are quite different for Oranges, the typical instruction formats can be difficult for them. In any learning environment, truly connecting with Orange children, and keeping them focused and interested is a special challenge, but well worth it.

Orange children excel when they learn through hands-on activities and making everything into a game or a contest, where they have the chance to become the winner. If not, being the class clown is often just as rewarding as being the class star. After all, attention is attention, whether positive or negative.

Orange children look for practical and direct instructions without a lot of details or rules. They seek instant and direct feedback and look for instructors who are flexible and innovative. This will be the children who routinely have their assignments incomplete, until the last minute. Written homework is an even bigger challenge because it does not give Oranges the chance to perform, or to improvise as they go along. As a result, homework assignments will often not be indicative of their knowledge or understanding of a subject as it is not a form of communication Oranges prefer.

To keep Orange children engaged and their fidgeting to a minimum, Abby Brown, a Minneapolis-St. Paul area teacher, had an idea. What if kids could be standing during her classes, instead of sitting? On her own initiative, she designed a stand-up desk for her Grade six class, and the results have been amazing. The quality of class work is up, marks are measurably improved, and schools throughout the country are beginning to use these desks.

Orange's favorite parts of school are social settings, including recess, dances, music, and drama, where Oranges can perform and or learn something practical, in their judgements. These are also areas where they can show off their creative skills and talents through the use of tools or acting. Orange children look for varied instructions and concrete activities that teach practical material and evaluate much of their learning in terms of *"what's in it for me?"*

Many school jurisdictions have now implemented privacy laws which prevent teachers from publishing marks, or singling out students for recognition. While there may be many valid reasons for these policies, it has become another area where the education system can leave Orange students behind. When teachers are not allowed to high-five an Orange student in class, a valuable motivation is taken away from this large group of students who are already the biggest at-risk group.

At times, many Orange kids can seem to become tired of *"fighting the system,"* as they see it, which may lead to a self-fulfilling prophecy. Dropping marks can lead to acting-out, which leads to a pressure to conform, and more discipline. This can result in mentally checking out and physically dropping out.

Make it a game and give me a chance
to win and I won't quit on you.

Green Children

Parents, get ready: Green children will become very independent, very quickly. It can seem as though there is now a mini-lawyer in the house since Green children ask a lot of probing questions, and will never settle for easy answers. These kids will also catch inconsistencies in answers, which keep their parents constantly on their toes. Their continuous questions will last a lifetime as will their never-ending quest for knowledge, understanding, and growth.

From the time Green children learn to read, or to log onto a computer, they value learning, puzzles, and figuring things out on their own. They are perfectly content being alone, and choose to have small circles of friends that share their joys of learning and exploring, and who can mentally challenge them.

A Green child is not likely to get involved in many social situations, and is perfectly comfortable alone. In later years, this independence will also apply to team sports and group activities where he or she may participate in some, but it will not become his or her preferred setting. It matters very little what other kids think, since Green children are the least likely to succumb to any peer pressure.

In school, Greens typically do not feel comfortable with many kids, lots of noise, and insufficient time to process or absorb material.

They value teaching styles which involve logical and well-planned presentations with opportunities for discussion and debates, and where they can ask lots of questions. Green children enjoy independently researching material and thrive on sharing what they have learned with others. Their favorite subjects are math, history, and science, or any areas involving complex problems or areas which stimulate their minds.

> Recently a Blue mother called, quite concerned about her Green daughter's math grades. In Grade 10, her final mark was a 95%. That was not a big surprise, as math tends to be one of Green's favorite subjects. Yet for the first half of her Grade 11 course, her daughter was barely passing. After just a few questions, it became clear that her daughter was convinced her math teacher "knows nothing about math."
>
> While her Blue mother did not want to think in those negative terms, her daughter had been sending a lot of signals that she could not get over the perceived lack of her teacher's credibility to focus on the course content. Without the maturity of an adult, or the tools of Colors, it was as though she wanted to prove the accuracy of her judgment. If she could simply study from home or in the library, her daughter would certainly get the same high marks at the end of the year while learning on her own. Even for teenagers, the Green need for credibility of others, and themselves, shows itself in many ways.

Green Learning Styles

Generally, Greens are among the quiet and intelligent group of students who focus on their studies without much desire for extra curricular matters. Green children seek to fully understand the basics, concepts, principles, and specifics of any subject. This includes simply having the time to digest and grasp the content of group discussions, or the chance to dissect the material in detail. The chance to wander off alone during breaks, into the library, or a quieter area of the room, allows them to process what they have learned, and to think through the material more thoroughly.

As the story on the previous page shows, of primary importance to Green children is the credibility of their instructors. They value teachers who are able to take the specific material and relate it to the big picture. Yes, at an early age, Green kids already look for credibility in people, processes, and study modules.

Green children love debates and discussions. During their lifetimes, there really are not many questions they do not want to ponder – the more complex, the better. Problem solving is almost a sport to Green children when they are mentally challenged and forced to think. Similar to workgroups of scientists or researchers, Greens thrive on this type of learning. When discussions happen with friends or others who they find credible, any Green child is very much in their element.

> *"…wondering about my eight year old who is trying to figure out how to make wireless electricity (because internet can be wireless)…but refuses to learn his 4 times tables!"* – M.H.M.

Making a Difference

These days, more than ever, it takes many special gifts and talents to be a teacher. There continues to be more and more pressure on our education system with rising expectations, many children with learning disabilities, and an increasing number for whom English is a second language. Added to that mix are different children with very different personality types, needs, and stresses. Being an effective teacher continues to become harder and more challenging.

Yet, in every school and every school district, there are countless numbers of teachers who find unique and creative ways to deal with all Colors of students in practical and effective ways:

By all accounts, Henry was one of the best teachers in his secondary school. He is Green/Gold. (Along with Gold/Green, it is the color combination of a large number of teachers). His classes consisted of more than 50 percent Orange students whose mind-set toward rules, deadlines, and being on time was quite the opposite of Henry's. Even decades ago, he started to realize that traditional learning styles were not going to reach these kids.

Through trial and error, Henry addressed both those issues in practical and easy ways that made him one of the school's favorite teachers. By incorporating the use of tools and lots of hands-on exercises and projects, these kids now had a chance to actively contribute in class.

An appropriate method of disciplining Orange students was always a challenge. The traditional method of sending them to the Principal's office had minimal effects on his students. In fact, to many it was almost a status symbol amongst their friends. It became more of a way of showing off, rather than one of accepting punishment. Henry's Green/Gold also wanted to deal with this challenge himself without simply passing the problem off to administrators. This reflected his strong Gold sense of accepting responsibility, and the strength of the Green mindset in looking at the big picture and finding an innovative solution.

But Henry needed to deal with the pent-up Orange energy of most of his students, their need to always be on the move, and their lack of proper school discipline. His solution was simple, yet powerful. "Get down and do 20 push-ups!" While his students were horrified at first, it soon became almost a game in his classes. It was an innovative solution which balanced the need for discipline with a very Orange chance to show off and do something physical.

To this day, Henry often runs into students who graduated decades ago. Some of them will still drop to the ground in the middle of a mall, and excitedly show off to Henry, and now their kids, that they can still do the 20 push ups. They were and are Orange, and although adults now, they still love to perform and show off to a teacher who made a measurable impact on their lives.

(The booklet: *The Colors of Parent and Child Dynamics* has many more extensive and in-depth insights into family dynamics, in addition to sections elaborating on every Color combination of parents and children.)

Eager to discuss new ideas
Diagnose the many difficulties you may face
Understand the potential of everyone
Communicate with them in their Colors
Accept them as they are, for each one is unique
Trust in what they thrive on
Improve on knowledge and understanding
Overbearing you should never be
Nudging gently to promote personal best

D. Erickson (adapted and used with permission)

Chapter Eleven

Self Esteem and Stress

Webster's dictionary defines self-esteem as *"holding in high regard,"* or *"to set a high value on, admire and respect."* When we live our life in harmony with our Colors, we grow our self-esteem and how we value our own worth. Bosses, parents, family, or friends can certainly point us in the right direction. They can always help and be supportive, but self-esteem is created within us. It grows by what we do and how we behave, through a sense of belonging and feeling valued, or by what we contribute to others. There are many ways to grow our self-esteem, but it always develops from within. It does not come from the verbal affirmations of others, but rather through our acts, behaviors, accomplishments, and feelings of empowerment.

When we live our lives in ways that feed our joys and values, this contributes to building our self-esteem. It grows and strengthens with each obstacle successfully tackled, with each accomplishment however small which we acknowledge as making a difference, or each time we reach out to touch the lives of others in positive ways.

> *"Don't undermine your self-worth by comparing*
> *yourself with others. It is because we are*
> *different that each of us is special."*
> Nancye Sims

We all strive to live and function in ways that reinforces our self-esteem and continuously grows us in positive ways. Being "in esteem" creates a feeling of being on top of the world. In our jobs, it becomes a feeling that we are really not working at all, but doing what we love to do – and it shows. It is often a state of mind where nothing gets to us. Fewer things become annoyances, and obstacles seem somehow much smaller and easier to tackle. The lows are not nearly as low, our attitude is relaxed, and things just seem to get better and better. In broad terms, having esteem translates to being authentic through being, and through living, as the people we really are. Self-esteem is how we feel about ourselves, irrespective of what others say, because it is the self-respect we earn for ourselves.

For Blues, their self-esteem grows through helping others, and having a part in making their world a little softer, more caring, and compassionate. When Blues find opportunities for team building in the office, having coffee with a friend who needs to talk, or volunteering their time and talents, their days become a lot brighter and more meaningful.

Golds derive a large part of their self-esteem through a deep seated sense of duty and responsibility. They esteem themselves by being of service as part of a team, committee, or group, and by contributing their organizational and planning skills. The Gold self-esteem is greatly enhanced when knowing they are organized and prepared, and when their plans are on track and unfolding the way they envision.

Greens esteem themselves through their power of knowledge and understanding. One of their primary drives is the constant search for information, improved processes, and focuses on the big picture. They place great value in attempting to understand almost everything around them and often look for opportunities to share their knowledge by teaching others. Greens value their logical thought processes and calm demeanors in pressure situations. They rely on their analytical abilities, which allow them to deal with complex or intricate problems. For Greens, it creates great joy when they are able to find solutions and answers in areas where most of the world has already given up.

Oranges build their self-esteem by being constantly active and retaining their freedom. Having lots on the go and constantly multi-tasking is their definition of a successful and fun day. They love the thrill of the sale, the chance to think on their feet, or direct hands-on involvement. Putting out fires, or dealing with immediate problems creates a real high for them, where others would certainly get stressed out. Oranges love being the center of attention and using their creative talents to find practical solutions for almost any challenge or obstacle.

You...
"Never be content with someone else's definition of you.
Instead, define yourself by your own beliefs, your own
truths, your own understanding of who you are, and
how you came to be. And never be content until
you are happy with the unique person you are!"
Author unknown

Measuring Success

Understanding our Colors allows each of us to discover our own unique strengths and definitions of success. Whether it is a specific event or a lifelong journey, success has very different definitions within the different Colors. It may be as simple as measuring a result in quantitative terms: making a budget, winning a sale, solving a specific problem, or completing everything on the to-do list.

In most instances, however, the measurement is not that simple or clear cut. Blues view success as spending part of their day listening to the needs of a friend, helping their team, serving clients, and knowing in their heart that they have made a small difference.

Or conversely, there may be times when Blues see that same day and think, "*I should have done more,*" which never contributes to building self-esteem. Blues will also never be the quantity group in any sales environment or call center, for example. They take the time to build meaningful relationships with clients. But what happens when a different Color boss looks only at the length of their call times, or the smaller number of appointments they have compared to other employees? What if they cannot see the loyalty and relationships Blues have created?

Our values can also be different from the priorities which society, or even our spouse or employer, can define for us. The key is not to measure our success against the scale, or Colors of others. Understanding this difference and choosing to measure our unique successes on our own personal scale is a foundation to building self-esteem.

Whatever people's Colors, their outlooks start with their attitudes and continue with positive judgments of their many accomplishments. When we focus on external views of success – at the expense of our own Color's definition – we become unhappy, stressed, and out of esteem.

Out of Esteem

Out of esteem can best be described as our dark side. It is often created when a Color lives with a large amount of self-doubt about who they really are, and also when their world has been turned upside down. It can come about through disharmony and conflict, or from family or work issues. Our self-esteem is diminished through insults or prejudices, hurt, anger, exclusion, or at times, just by feeling unloved.

Out of esteem has a direct connection to being under stress. However, just as self-esteem is reached in different ways for each

Color, out of esteem is also very different for each group. In fact, one Color's self-esteem builder and joy, often has the exact opposite effect on another Color.

For Oranges, the great thrill is to multi-task and to stay crazy busy. This is done to simply avoid getting bored, and it creates great variety and a huge adrenaline rush. To Golds, having a number of things on the go and adding more stuff onto their list – while nothing is getting finished – creates the opposite effect. Their esteem is built through closure and finishing a task. Golds love the completed to-do list while their Orange friends find them boring. Both of these examples show quite a different view of a very similar day.

If we understand how we behave when we are out of esteem, it often reduces stressful situations before they can escalate. Being aware of the oncoming warning signs leads us to a deeper understanding of ourselves and others. It frequently gives us powerful clues to actions, reactions, or trigger points. After all, we cannot change or heal what we do not acknowledge and hurting people hurt other people.

Blue Out of Esteem

Out of esteem behaviors for Blues exhibit themselves in very uncharacteristic ways. In this state, being around people actually becomes a stress. Blues frequently discount (or do not make it their priority) to take care of themselves, in order to take care of others. They start feeling that nobody cares about them, or that they never really do enough. Also in this state, Blues will become overly emotional and cry for extended periods of time. The Blue tendency of taking care of others often helps them to avoid their own situations and issues. These are just times when Blues reach overload and things blow up.

Out of esteem causes Blues to feel truly alone, as though almost no one loves them or really cares. Their difficulty in asking for anything for themselves and their inability to say no can reach a state of semi-depression. After all, they feel that any act of selfishness may mean others might not like them anymore. At that point, out of esteem can manifest itself through visible anger, such as yelling, or acting out.

Anger turned inward becomes depression. Before verbalizing their feelings, many Blues will bite their tongue for quite some time. In that depressed or hurt state, comfort food can become a reliable go-to "friend." Unfortunately, comfort foods will probably not be fruits or vegetables. This "friend" may then become a frequent source of weight gain while Blues hide from the world and attempt to suppress their feelings.

The Blue out-of-esteem state can also create large selfish streaks for short periods of time. After having bent and stretched to the wishes of others for so long, Blues can turn to the opposite extreme of selfishness. In some instances they may exhibit very passive-aggressive behavior, or perhaps withdraw altogether.

Other Blue out of esteem behaviors:

Acting phony-nice	Anxious or anxiety attacks
Becoming judgmental	Blaming others
Crying	Dropping out
Emotionally numb, shut down	Extreme people-pleasing
Feeling useless	Getting-even mindset
Indecision	Losing sense of reasoning
Over-eating or starving	Over-reacting
Overwhelmed by problems	Vindictive
Withdrawn, avoiding people	Yelling/aggressive behavior

Gold Out of Esteem

When Golds are out of esteem, their usual concerned demeanor turns quite negative. They will over plan and over prepare to the nth degree and display visible signs of anxiety, stress, and worry. In a drive to do more, and to do better, Golds are already quite hard on themselves. In this state, their criticism turns outward onto others. These include verbal criticisms, visible impatience, or harsh judgments. Their black or white mindset can become even more defined with a tendency to turn more rigid and strict in their behaviors.

Golds generally work towards closure and getting things done. When they are out of esteem, Golds can simply quit on something to put the matter behind them. It becomes a *"what's the use"* or *"what's the point trying"* type of attitude. This mindset can also extend to trouble in relationships, or giving up on their jobs. At some point, they just simply want their troubles to be over with. If that means quitting, so be it – at least they believe they will reach closure in order to move forward. It may be self-destructive, or over-reacting, but in these times, Golds believe they will at least get their problems behind them.

When things turn bad, Golds often avoid relying on others and, instead, become solo performers. They may take on more and more work, which generally makes things worse, instead of better. Other signals are a noticeable state of fatigue and depression, where Golds just want to hide at home or in bed until their problems have gone away. Frequently, this is brought on by simply getting burned out. At that point, Golds re-live their view of how much they have done for others, and the countless times they have helped above and beyond the call of duty, yet how little help, cooperation, or gratitude they have actually received. When Golds are out of esteem, they can exhibit noticeable signs of feeling sorry for themselves, and seek ways of eliciting sympathy from others.

Other Gold out of esteem behaviors:

Abrupt & short

Defensive & blaming

Hiding through workaholic
  mindset

Making others feel guilty/lazy

Nobody does anything right

Over-perfecting & preparing

Stressing over little things

Seeing only negatives, faults
  and problems

Total control

Confrontational

Following rules blindly

Losing sleep

Micro-managing others

Not doing enough or never
  good enough

Strict lists & schedules

Zero tolerance for getting
  off track or off task

Orange Out of Esteem

Our Orange friends look to stay on a natural high in life. If that cannot be accomplished in constructive ways, substance abuse can become an alternative. Oranges are, unfortunately, the largest group of substance abusers. Out of esteem behaviors can include the use of alcohol, drugs, or gambling. These never create the same high as positive accomplishments, but only act as temporary substitutes. Oranges can also start to act out, or behave quite rudely. They may lash out and purposely break rules and policies, or their high physical energy can turn to visible anger which may even escalate to violence.

Revenge is also something that goes through the minds of Oranges when they are out of esteem. They may display an over-whelming sense of anger, and a desire to get even. In this state, Oranges may use information they remember about someone and turn it against the person in an effort to lash out and be hurtful. Their great thrill of making things happen may also turn to paralysis. It is a state where

Oranges avoid, or delay decisions, and become serious procrastinators. There is one final, regretful behavior, where they will simply quit or walk away. In relationships or in their jobs, Oranges are capable of making a snap decision and simply walk. As the Johnny Paycheck song says, *"Take this job and shove it."*

Other Orange out of esteem behaviors:

Avoidance & procrastination

Get them before they get me

Inappropriate humor/comments

Not honoring commitments

Put downs & cheap shots

Rolling eyes & clear
  facial expressions

"Whatever" or "who cares" attitude

Forgive but never resolve

Hit & run arguments

"I was just kidding" attitude

Physically intimidating

Revenge or getting even

Rubbing it in

Green Out of Esteem

Out of esteem behavior for Greens is generally only noticeable in subtle ways. Since their usual calm, cool, and collected demeanor shows very little in their facial expressions, it often manifests itself verbally. The most observable outward expressions are through sarcastic, sharp, or judgmental comments. Greens certainly have an extensive vocabulary and sharp wit. During these times, their tongues and sarcasm can become dangerous weapons.

When they are out of esteem, Greens will likely withdraw further from interacting with anyone and everyone. They become even quieter and "hide" in their minds. They may also exhibit signs of stubbornness, which can show in their refusal to cooperate with anyone about anything. Their critical nature becomes exacerbated even further.

At times, the Green mind goes through waves of second-guessing many of life's decisions. These flashbacks focus on both current problems, but also issues which go back many years, where Greens re-live, re-think, and re-analyze these events and issues.

With current projects, this over-analyzing can become a period of paralysis. It puts Greens into a state of not making any decisions at all. This lack of decision making will not be a result of any lack of information or time, but this state of second-guessing and freezing will prevent them from moving forward. Alternately, they may become focused exclusively on one issue, which can consume their thought processes.

Other Green out of esteem behaviors:

A "needing more information" addiction	Condescending
	Cynical or sarcastic
Defensive	Extreme right vs. happy attitude
Freezing on decisions	
Increasing frustration level	More & more alone time
Over-thinking/analyzing	
Proving "I'm right" *and* "you're stupid"	Rapid fire questions
Shutting down or withdrawing	Stubborn and/or entrenched
Waves of second-guessing	

All of us know when we have reached our limits. Being aware of the early-warning signals helps us to become aware of this sooner, rather than later – before it escalates into a serious problem or blows up very publicly. For every Color, there are examples of taking things too far (way too far), when specific trigger points are reached after being out of esteem for extended periods of time:

An excellent Gold lounge manager of a well-known restaurant chain was responsible for a huge increase in volume during his first year. While he worked with a large group of Orange staff, he was able to keep his "right" way of organizing the lounge in check and under control. But when someone went into "his" tool drawer for the third time and didn't return a hammer to the "right" place, he lost it. The scene he made about something so trivial in the big picture of life actually got him fired.

A very public Orange example of taking the spotlight to extremes was the reported meltdown of football pro Terrell Owens. Owens believed that not enough attention was paid to him after his touchdown receptions. At one point he went public – very public, with his displeasure by lashing out at his teammates. Shortly afterwards, the Eagles suspended Owens and subsequently traded him to the Dallas Cowboys who also gave up on him. One newspaper headline read: "A *Talking Injury Sidelines Owens.*"

Out of esteem behaviors should always act as warning signals or calls for help. Since every person is a unique combination of Colors, many actions and behaviors can overlap, or manifest themselves in a multitude of other ways. Depending on the circumstances, or someone's state of mind, being out of esteem can be resolved quickly, or can linger for months. In either event, every person can use a hand and a friend.

There are also a number of self-help books that may be of assistance, as is a powerful seminar called Choices, which everyone deserves to experience. (choicesseminars.com.) When out of esteem behaviors persist, or deepen, taking the time to visit with a professional is another excellent tool to use sooner, rather than later, for specific, focused, and often invaluable help.

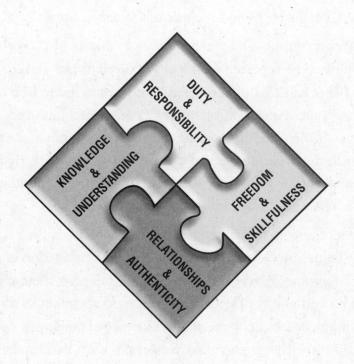

Chapter Twelve

The Last Word

Throughout each and every chapter of this book are literally hundreds of insights into each of our Colors.

There is no better or worse Color. There is no combination of our Colors superior to any other. There is also no team or office which would become more successful if there were only three more of this Color, or two less of that one. And in our relationships, every combination of Colors is ideal, because love is always colorblind.

Yet all of it starts with an open heart, an open mind, and the insights of our Colors. We can begin to spend more time looking for what we have in common instead of looking at our differences. Finally, to value and appreciate the positives and the blessings of each of our Colors:

The Colors of the World

Once upon a time the colors of the world started to quarrel. All claimed that they were the best, the most important, the most useful.

Green said: "Clearly I am the most important. I am the sign of life and of hope. I was chosen for grass, trees, and leaves. Without me, all animals would die. Look over the countryside and you will see that I am in the majority."

Blue retorted: "You only think about the earth, but consider the sky and the sea. It is the water that is the basis of life and drawn up by the clouds from the deep sea. The sky gives space and peace and serenity. Without my peace, you would all be nothing."

Yellow chuckled: "You are all so serious. I bring happiness and warmth into the world. The sun is yellow, the moon is yellow, and the stars are yellow. Every time you look at a sunflower, the whole world starts to smile. Without me there would be no joy."

Orange started next to blow her trumpet: "I am the color of health and strength. I may be scarce, but I am precious for I serve the needs of human life. I carry the most important vitamins. Think of carrots, pumpkins, oranges, mangoes, and papayas. I don't hang around all the time, but when I fill the sky at sunrise or sunset, my beauty is so striking that no one gives another thought to any of you."

And so the colors went on boasting, each convinced of his or her own superiority. Their quarreling became louder and louder. Suddenly there was a startling flash of bright lightening, and thunder rolled and boomed. Rain started to pour down relentlessly. The colors crouched down in fear, drawing close to one another for comfort.

In the midst of the clamor, rain began to speak: "You foolish colors, fighting amongst yourselves, each trying to dominate the rest. Don't you know that you were each made for a special purpose, unique and different? Join hands with one another and come to me."

Doing as they were told, the colors united and joined hands. The rain continued: "From now on, when it rains, each of you will stretch across the sky in a great bow of color as a reminder that you can all live in peace. So whenever a good rain washes the world, and a Rainbow appears in the sky let us remember to appreciate one another."

— Author unknown

Your Beautiful Picture

Have you ever received a picture from a young child? It's usually a picture torn out of a coloring book, with vivid colors scrawled all over the page, in and out of the lines.

Our expressions at such a gift often range into wonder rather than simple thanks. We are thrilled at the heartfelt gift and recognize that one day this picture will change. More colors will be added, patterns will develop, but no picture later will please us any more than this gift we've just been given.

You see, God doesn't expect a perfect picture and He doesn't expect you to understand it fully, or to use every color He has created. He couldn't care that you drew inside the lines or not and He will always understand that special scrawl in the corner drawn just for Him. He could not be more pleased and He could not love it any more. Each of our lives is that picture to God — that rough and unique gift that each of us draws very differently.

We never consider that our young friend is upset that their picture isn't perfect. That they could have made us just a little more pleased if their picture had more technique. Don't ever beat yourself up over a part of your life you thought you could have done better. Don't ever consider hiding it from Him that created you entirely as you are.

All we have to do to make God happy is to give Him our gift as it is — as we are. He understands that we do not have the perfect picture and that we will not always succeed, but He simply asks that we try and accept our picture just as we drew it.

— Sarah Rudd – used with permission

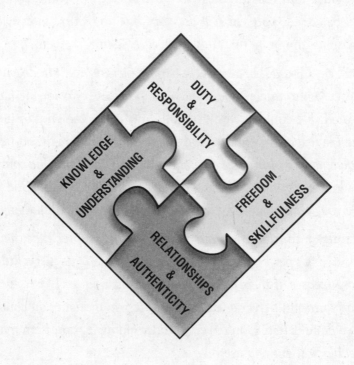

A Note From the Author

Anyone who has already attended a Colors seminar has experienced first-hand the vast difference between reading a book and living the training. It brings the material to life in three-dimensional ways with tools that last a lifetime. I would invite you to make that a goal in your life and with your team for this coming year.

Just imagine the positive changes if everyone simply understood us a little better, with the tools and knowledge to speak our language, celebrate our differences, and value us just the way we are.

George J. Boelcke, CCP
www.vantageseminars.com

George Boelcke, CCP is President of Vantage Consulting. As author, speaker, and frequent media guest, he facilitates seminars on personality types, relationships, sales, and team-building throughout North America and Europe for groups ranging from Fortune 500 companies to conferences, sales teams and church groups.

George is the author of this bestseller, as well as: *The Colors of Relationships, Colors Tools for Christians, The Colors of Leadership and Management, Sales and Customers,* and *Parent & Child Dynamics.*

The Colors Self-Assessment

Score each group of words, for all eight questions, on a scale of:

    4 – which is the most like you

    3 – which is quite a bit like you

    2 – which is a little bit like you

    1 – which is the least like you

      (Each question can have only one score of 1, one 2, one 3 and one 4)

1. a) _____ compassion, sharing, sympathetic
   b) _____ duty, detailed, traditions
   c) _____ verbal, risk-taker, promoter
   d) _____ rational, knowledge, visionary

2. a) _____ feelings, meaningful, cooperation
   b) _____ conservative, reliable, stability
   c) _____ spontaneous, generous, action
   d) _____ credibility, focused, probing

3. a) _____ authentic, encouraging, spiritual
   b) _____ devoted, cautious, status-quo
   c) _____ surprises, freedom, short-cuts
   d) _____ inventive, principled, competence

4. a) _____ unique, sensitive, peace-maker
   b) _____ steady, planning, loyal
   c) _____ open-minded, playful, hands-on
   d) _____ curious, determined, rational

5. a) ____ tender, involved, connecting

   b) ____ lists, procedural, responsible

   c) ____ competitive, outgoing, direct

   d) ____ exploring, skeptical, complex

6. a) ____ devoted, caring, self-improvement

   b) ____ dependable, structured, belonging

   c) ____ flexible, daring, persuasive

   d) ____ independent, perfectionist, reserved

7. a) ____ intuition, sharing, positive

   b) ____ orderly, honor, rule-follower

   c) ____ immediate, skillful, active

   d) ____ theoretical, calm & cool, learning

8. a) ____ affectionate, accommodating, harmony

   b) ____ private, serious, moral

   c) ____ networking, adventure, winning

   d) ____ analytical, logical, improving

Your total score for:

a) Blue ____ b) Gold ____ c) Orange ____ d) Green ____

(The total of your four scores will equal 80)